My Mamiya made me a Million.

THE ESSENTIAL GUIDE
TO TURNING PROFESSIONAL.

This book is dedicated to
Ernest Cogman and Aircrew,
who gave their lives
that we might live.

A Successful Photographer Reveals His Secrets

My Mamiya made me a Million.

THE ESSENTIAL GUIDE TO TURNING PROFESSIONAL.

Keith Cogman

First Published 1991

ISBN 0-9517916-0-5

Photoset in Plantin
Printed by Jolly & Barber Ltd, Rugby, Warwickshire

Cartoons by 'Russ'

Published by Zirconium
PO Box 230, Coventry CV5 8PJ

CONTENTS

With Grateful thanks to:

Russ, cartoonist extraordinaire
Arthur Cogman, for his friendship and faith
Veronica, for all those gallons of tea
Paul Dibbens, for being generous with his time
Jaffir Bhatti, and friends; for asking questions

never forgetting,

Isabel McCulloch, script-reader; for her precise Scottish ways, and for cracking the whip and *trying* to discipline me. (Nobody should mind being criticised by someone who 'knows a lot better than what they do').

A special 'Thank You' to Colab Limited and all their Staff, for their patience and caring over so many years.

With grateful thanks to The Mamiya Camera Co. Ltd., who did nothing, except make a fine camera system.

"MY MAMIYA MADE ME A MILLION"

"For The Record... The 'Mamiya' Connection"

Despite the alliterative title, this book is not an account of my 'adventures' with Mamiya cameras, although together we've certainly had our moments, my camera and I.

The book is much more than that. It is the first manual of its kind, structured to help all would-be professionals, and bridge the yawning gap that exists between the accomplished amateur and established professional photographers. It is my belief that the differences are minimal and mostly down to an attitude of mind and lack of experience of professional work. I believe those differences can be eradicated, hence the book, which at the outset was going to be called "Making It", referring to 'making it' in the professional sense and of making lots of money in the process, but I decided it was too obscure a title, and perhaps a little too clever. The book had been almost five years in the writing, so there was no hurry to finalise the title!

The eventual title came about as a result of a visit to a photographic exhibition where I was keeping myself up-to-date with new developments in the photographic world.

Whilst looking at the latest Mamiyas, the conversation came around to my own cameras and it was suggested that, as I was the owner of one of the first Mamiya 645's, the camera had probably paid for itself by now. That caused me a wry smile, because I knew it had, many times over!

Back at my studio I decided to do some simple arithmetic and, frankly, I was amazed at the final figures. The camera in question was 20 years old and during that time the average annual turnover had been in excess of £50,000, most of it during the last ten years, and all down to one camera. I thought I had got one too many 'zeros' at first and double-checked my results. Sure enough, £1,000,000, and still growing daily!

My first feelings of incredulity were quickly replaced by those of 'guilt' and 'pride', in that order.

Guilt because it wasn't something I should like my clients to find out about, in case they thought my 'old' camera should be pensioned-off, and I had been trading without any "equipment overheads". How could I justify my professional prices using 20 year old gear? I generally like to keep a low profile, so decided to keep my secret.

Certainly I was proud, in a sense. Proud of looking after my equipment so well that nobody could tell its age by looking at it but, I decided, much of the credit must go to Mamiya and whoever designed and made the camera all those years ago.

The revelations didn't end there. My memory for some things is 'photographic' and, because I had been personally responsible for the camera and its lenses during that 20 year period, I knew all it had gone through.

Medium-format cameras are extremely versatile and can be used for almost any assignment, both in the studio and on location. My own camera has been used in just about every conceivable situation, including fast studio-strobe glamour photography, portraiture, architecture, industrial and commercial, interiors, medical and, extensively for aerial photography. More recently, specialising in brochure work covering a multitude of subjects for some very discerning art directors. During all this time, it has travelled almost a million miles with me, in all weathers. Strangely, during its busy life, it is I who have aged, but the camera still looks very much the same!

Perhaps even more amazing, the camera has never let me down. Nothing has fallen off and it has never even been serviced (unless you call a blow-through with compressed air a 'service'). I've always worked on the premise "If it's all working, leave well alone". Most professionals are like that. Perhaps I should add to 'guilt' and 'pride' the word 'shame' – for neglecting it!

The title is, I hope, a fitting tribute to a faithful old friend who has shared my life for so long. But the first that Mamiya (the camera-people in Japan) knew of this book was in the Spring of 1991 when I respectfully asked for their permission to use the name in the title. They still don't know the contents of these pages because my words are all my own, always preferring to operate independently in everything I do.

I can't see them objecting to my totally unsolicited testimonial. The only link I have with Mamiya is my own personal relationship with a fine camera. Credit where credit is due.

Keith Cogman

CHAPTER ONE.

Introduction...to a new way of life.

This is not another book on how to take photographs, there are already enough of those to fill a fair-sized library, and their numbers are growing almost daily. These are often written by armchair photographers or commissioned authors relying on, and based upon, the excellent textbooks of authors such as John Hedgecoe or Michael Langford.

However, if we read enough of these volumes, we can grasp the techniques involved in the taking of decent photographs but, from there on, you are on your own. Students wishing to embark upon a career in photography are left to their own devices when it comes to things like pricing, finding work, self-promotion and other essential aspects of business management. For some strange reason, there always seems to have been a great gaping void where some real help is needed. This book should go some way towards redressing the situation.

I soon became aware, in the freshness of my youth as an aspiring photographer, of the unwillingness of other photographers to share their knowledge, not just with me but, apparently, with anyone. This was something I had to come to terms with and, although I could not understand it, I could see the reasons why. The accomplished amateur feared that his 'student' might end up knowing more than he, or perhaps his own knowledge might be revealed as inaccurate or insufficient if subjected to close scrutiny. The professional also seemed to have no time for the likes of me either, with his aloof disdain based upon his pride and insecurity. Surely he couldn't think I would ever be a threat to his livelihood? Both amateur and professional choosing to confuse my questions with over-complicated jargon that was intended to put me in my place.

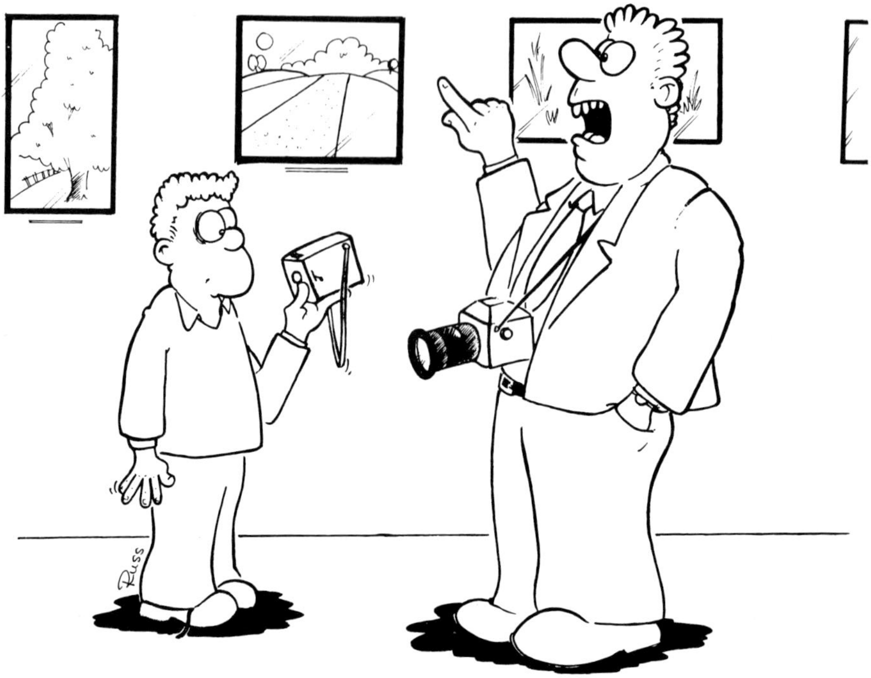

Naturally I meant neither any harm, only seeking to improve my own then-sparse knowledge on the subject of taking pictures. After many snubs and rebuffs, I eventually got the message and, vowing never to be that way myself, proceeded to glean as much information as I could from books, and from personal experimentation and practical experience.

Some might say this is the best way, and I wouldn't argue with that as an option, but it is extremely time consuming. Who can afford to be practically middle-aged before claiming to be expert in their field? Unfortunately, I was blessed with patience. I say "unfortunately" because, when you are a teenager, you think you will live forever, time is on your side. Ten years of self-training didn't seem such an ordeal at the time but, ten years soon became twenty, and so on. Many older people surely look back and say to themselves,

"I had no idea it would take so long, and here I am still striving to accomplish".

Speaking for myself, I simply wish there had been somebody, just anybody, who understood and was willing to give me the time of day, and the help I needed so badly. So I eventually learned my craft the hard way, by making mistakes, taking two steps forward and one back until, after many years of trials and tribulations, I made a breakthrough.

Not a technical breakthrough, you understand, more a dawning of the realisation that success in professional photography wasn't all technique as I had thought. The act of taking the photograph was of minor importance compared to all the other things. It was the 'other things' that made the difference between rich and poor, success and failure!

Sure, it was necessary to get sharp, correctly exposed and nicely composed pictures, but is that so difficult? The real secret lies in attitudes, ideas, confidence, planning, caring and composure. Self-image can enhance images, and there is a psychology to professional photography that opens doors, allowing us all do it, given the formula. That formula can not only improve your life in photography, but can give a similar level of achievement and advancement in your personal life too.

Throughout this book two words keep cropping up with some regularity. Success and achievement. It is difficult to express these goals in any other way so, as far as I'm concerned, they will do. Almost from birth we are motivated by the pursuance of these targets. As we learn to talk, walk and, eventually, to run to school, we cannot escape them. The goals are always there, like dangling carrots, keeping us motivated and sometimes, as dreams, out of reach except in our imaginations. Yet there are those amongst us who seem to waltz through life as if blessed in some way, and perhaps they are. Others, on their deathbeds, bemoan the fact that they had so much to do, and had so little time, still conscious of the fact they had acted too late to achieve their life's ambitions.

Personal satisfaction and status in this world seem to be measured by the degree of success achieved. Our aims in life are put against this metaphorical yardstick to measure up, and be judged. Happiness and bank balances are synonymous with achievements, and even our cars reflect our status and can affect how we are perceived by others – and eventually our children fall to the same trap.

Yet there are things we can do to hasten progress in our chosen field, if only we are shown the way. In professional photography we must appreciate that technical ability is only linked with success, not the reason for it.

If we take the trouble to think about it, the critical factors separating the successful from the unsuccessful are really quite basic.

A surgeon, for instance, needs dexterity and the ability to enable him to perform his job, based upon learning standard techniques. He also needs the equipment necessary for him to carry out those skills, an inquiring mind to keep him informed and up-to-date with new techniques and improvisational skills. If those criteria are all present, it leaves only one vital ingredient. Confidence, and the balls to use all his experience and knowledge, to effect successful operations. It's that vital ingredient that decides whether our surgeon will be successful and respected, or otherwise. The buck stops with him, as it does with any professional photographer. And the similarities don't end there. Armed with his knowledge and some equipment, he tackles his problems on a day-to-day basis, being flexible enough to improvise should it be necessary. He knows his job, but can only be successful if he has the confidence in his ability and the equipment that is so vital to his success. This is professionalism in action!

To become 'a professional', for most people, is just a dream. This is simply because they are not armed with the necessary inside information that separates the keen amateur from the successful professional. The main ingredient missing is, of course, experience. Experience breeds confidence, confidence means success, and success usually leads to financial reward.

Did I hear you say you can't gain real experience without growing old in the process? And that we're not on this Earth long enough to wait twenty years for recognition? True!!

You don't really want to wait until middle-age before driving your Porsche, though most people have to. Middle-aged people say "Youth is wasted on the young.", simply because they feel they now have the wealth of their experience to enjoy their youth much more than they did when it was their turn. They may be right, but shortcuts can be made. People who take shortcuts reach their destinations quicker, either because they took a chance or because they had inside information.

Life isn't a school cross-country run where you are penalised for cutting corners, life is about goal-seeking and achievement, there isn't always time to take the long way round. And, from my experience, that isn't always the prettiest route either.

Ambitious young people used to queue up to work for David Bailey (and maybe still do), wanting no wages, simply to be near to their idol. No matter how menial the position, to be in his company was enough, to learn all they could from this acknowledged 'master' who was so young, yet so successful, in the hope that, perhaps, some of his secrets would rub off on them; that one day they too might be revered.

You have probably heard of the modern-day problem where it is impossible to get a job because you have no experience, but you can't get experience without getting a job. This is known as a 'catch 22' situation and, to some degree, it applies to thousands of aspiring young people who have the technical ability to become good photographers but can't 'break in' to the profession. Sadly, less than one in ten would-be photographers ever make a living at it, and then often in a very small way, living from day-to-day, surviving on the odd wedding and small-time commercial work, hoping that around the corner something will happen to change the situation. Usually the only thing around the corner is another corner and eventually they are forced by financial circumstances to take up a 'proper' job.

In other words, working for somebody else on a regular basis for regular pay. Another dream shattered and around him, or her, valid reasons why it didn't work out. Almost without exception the reasons for failure revolve around the following circumstances;

a) Lack of contacts

b) Not enough capital outlay, or poor management

c) Too much competition from established professionals

d) Lack of confidence (few admit this one), and a fear of failing.

e) Not enough work in the area

f) Lack of experience (the biggest single factor)

These are all-too-obvious reasons when you see them listed, but few can truthfully say they have never suffered those fears or phobias themselves. Not even fully-fledged professionals, though it's easy to criticise when you've 'made it' yourself. Naturally, along the road to success many mistakes are made, particularly when there is no-one you can turn to for guidance. Everyone can learn from their mistakes, but isn't it far less painful to learn from the mistakes of others? And that is just what you are going to do!

You are going to expand your knowledge and gain from mistakes made by others on their way up, and from the store of my own experiences and those of people just like me. This I give freely (apart from the cost of this book). And to those people who want to know *why* I won't jealously guard my secrets, or those of my fellow-professionals, I say RUBBISH! There's plenty to go around, and sharing the cake is, in my opinion, a better way to conduct your life than sneaking around peeling an orange in your pocket with one hand whilst shaking somebody else's hand with the other. Let's not forget, almost all professional photographers were once amateurs!

I realise, now that my book is written, that there will be criticism of my methods and of my style, but every word is designed to inform the uninitiated, from the humblest snap-shooter merely eager to gain an insight into the profession, to the most serious professional anxious to compare notes with another photographer's 'modus operandi'. Yes, there are secrets, of a sort, and some would say that I've taken the lid off the mystique to a degree but, in my own simplistic way, I have been driven by a real personal need to put professional photography into perspective. If we didn't learn from those who have gone before, then how could man hope to make progress? We would simply keep making the same mistakes over and over, generation after generation!

In our search for 'the truth', we look at the many and varied topics of major concern for would-be professionals. I have attempted to weave questions and answers into the fabric of each paragraph, sometimes unashamedly throwing facts and trade secrets about like confetti and, at other times, simply giving the reader ample food for thought so that he might make some of his own discoveries within these pages. I also use some psychology in the knowledge that, in this profession, it is very much a question of developing the correct mental attitude, and sometimes use parable in order to give examples of human nature and the way in which it can affect our business.

Most of all, this book picks up where all other self-help photographic books stop short. It doesn't contain the usual padding of pretty pictures normally associated with how-to-do-it photography books, even though my critics say it should. My single most important aim and objective is to fill those gaps in your knowledge so far denied you, to enable you to think and feel like a professional photographer. Then if you decide "you must, you can, and you will", at least you will have a much better start than I ever had.

We shall be looking closely at all the 'favourite' phobias of young professionals, showing how such fears can be eradicated. There are whole chapters dedicated to certain topics essential to sales, customer-care and self-promotion, with a strong emphasis on money-management, and not forgetting solving the perennial headache of realistic pricing and professional fees. There is, of course, full instructions on how to earn an average of £1000 per week, and true-life examples of how, *single-handedly*, I have regularly made £1000 per day! You will be shown how it is possible to make money you hitherto thought was an impossible dream! I will go on to tell you how to look after your money and how to spend it wisely, because you should know that too!

Furthermore, to fulfil previous promises to certain students, I have included several 'bonus' sections dealing with vital issues such as how to get 'Creative'; 'Meeting People'; 'Sun, Wind and Weather' and how it affects us as photographers, and much more besides.

Why have a whole chapter devoted to Sun, Wind and Weather when we all know the sun comes up every morning, sometimes it's windy and sometimes it isn't, and often there are fluffy things floating in the sky called clouds? Well, such simple knowledge may be enough for the majority of people, but a photographer's life can be ruled by the elements, therefore our understanding has to be much deeper if we wish to maximise our earning powers.

I love teaching. Passing on information gives me great satisfaction and writing this book seems a better and a more permanent way of reaching a much greater audience than I could ever hope to reach in a lifetime of lecturing. We shall be looking at the many aspects of taking up photography as a profession, mostly based on personal experience and, of course, answering those favourite queries my students continually bombard me with. At all times the journey will be made as painless as possible, forever mindful that the reader may be either a student or perhaps a more mature person wishing to relocate.

Despite a externally lofty air, I really don't consider myself as anything other than an experienced operator. I am not especially gifted in any artistic way, but I do have my strengths. I write within this book about a genuine caring attitude towards your client and his needs, and that is vital.

Good technique is also most desirable, with a constant eye on quality all along the line; that is expected, and separates the well-paid professional from the amateur. High among the attributes I would least like to lose (for business and personal reasons) I include the following. There is no question that appearing 'cool' and calm, when all around you are losing their heads, is a priceless asset and it's all an attitude of mind to be acquired by any who desire it. The recipe is quite simple, it is not a gift but a knack to be learned, and later reinforced, by practice.

That quiet confidence necessary to 'be the part' stems from a thorough understanding of the tools of your trade.

1. Know your equipment inside out, including filters, and their uses.
2. Become familiar with all films and their respective uses.
3. Experiment with balancing ambient light with flash, direct or bounced.
4. Know and trust your meters; or trade them in.

Having those four practical skills are the reasons why most prospective clients pay for your services. But you are to be *more* than just a photographer, you are soon to be a confident one; that's what will set you apart from most others.

When you have mastered the basics, and that's not a tall order for any aspiring professional, you are ready for phase two.

Phase two; to know your job and keep pace with new ideas and technology, always seeking ways for self-improvement.

At the end of the day, the key word is 'motivation', and here we have the greatest incentive known to man. To succeed. According to my dictionary, success is defined as 'achieving a level of honour in life that prompts respect from others'. Though it is the trappings of success that most people find so attractive; that of financial security and a comfortable lifestyle. Or maybe even fame!

For others, it is enough to reach a goal, to achieve. When a modest man *achieves* success, he honestly can't see what the fuss is about. He feels no different though, to others, he is. Perhaps in his new wisdom, he knows that it is not the end of the struggle, merely a stepping stone. And his next goal will come easier, giving more time to help others find their feet.

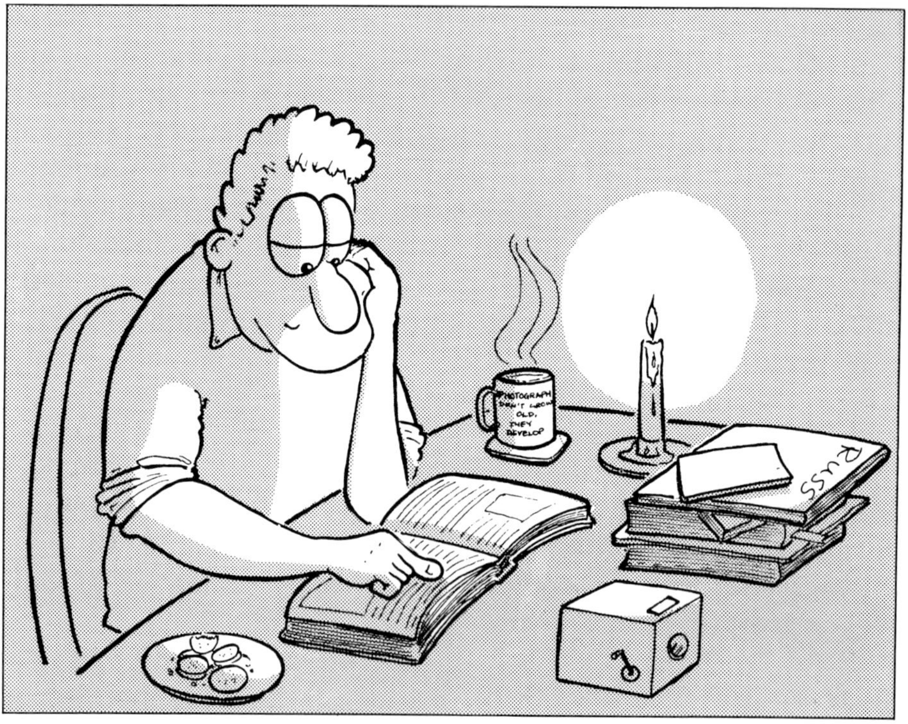

A Long Way To Go!

As a young photographer, with all of six years experience behind me, I had a regular assignment in a neighbouring town photographing shop-window displays. Dutifully, I always arrived on time and went through my routine, which usually involved a couple of black and white views taken at dusk to avoid unwanted reflections in the plate-glass window. The trick was to catch it when the daylight level had fallen sufficiently to balance with the artificial light of the display.

I remember I used to try to make my 'skills' look as clever and mysterious as possible (to justify my title of 'professional'), making much of focussing the 5 × 4 plate camera, often lingering under the magic black and red focussing cloth much longer than really necessary, all whilst crossing and rising the front lens panel, whether it was necessary or not.

In honesty the hardest part about this type of work was ensuring the camera-back was perfectly vertical, and parallel with the vertical plane of the window, particularly when using a wide angle lens, because a few degrees out of true meant correcting the converging verticals later on the enlarger. I almost always took two exposures, veering on the over-exposure side, and developed accordingly. I went through my routine, always being methodical and conscientious (though I say so myself) and with perhaps a little too much pride for one so young – perhaps over-compensating for my youth in the presence of my grey-haired client.

He was a kindly person who had tolerated me well on every occasion and had said he enjoyed photography himself as a hobby. At our previous meeting he had mentioned his interest in photographing churches and I don't deny I winced at the thought of him pulling out his holiday snaps. However, my employer was an old friend of his (hence the job) so I had to be courteous to a fault, whether I felt like it or not.

As previously promised, he had brought along some pictures he had taken, and as I packed away my MPP camera he invited me into the shop, for a cup of coffee to thaw us out. Once there he fished out an old box full of prints that seemed big enough to bore me for hours.

"I'm afraid I'm no professional", he apologised. "I've a long way to go yet but I do enjoy my photography, especially the interiors of churches". "Oh God!" I thought.

"Perhaps you would be good enough to give me a few pointers?" he said modestly, as he opened the battered box.

There sitting on top of a pile of mounted prints was an extremely sharp, perfectly graduated, sepia print. The vertical lines of the church interior were vertical, the shadow detail exquisite and, if he had shaded-up the stained-glass windows and rays of sunlight that poured down the nave, I certainly couldn't tell!

I tried not to gasp, or look too awe-struck, but I swallowed a bit as I slowly went through his collection one by one, listening to the modest man's commentary as he recalled what special lighting problems he had overcome. Mainly, it involved going at just the right time of day, with careful exposure and development technique based upon "exposing for the shadows and developing for the highlights", he said. And mentioned some fellow called "Watkins Factor".

The camera he had used for the last thirty years was an old wooden Sanderson half-plate. This rickety relic he kept immaculately clean, never taking it out of it's crafted case unless he intended to use it. (A bit like a Samurai sword, you might say, or a Gurkha knife). Maybe he treated it so reverently because he respected its power. He had certainly mastered all it's capabilities and, judging from his work which was carefully cropped and beautifully mounted, he had overtaken me, technically, many years previous.

Naturally, I tried to say all the right things and joined in with his enthusiasm, eventually thanking him as I left his company (and the coffee, which was terrible), somehow much wiser now.

That day I learned the meaning of humility. And also how we should not pre-judge so-called 'amateurs'. If we are fortunate enough to do for a living what others do for pleasure then we owe it to ourselves, and those that employ us, to give a little extra effort to our work. Striving to achieve, and to overcome all technical barriers so that one day we might say we *are* professionals, and actually believe it ourselves. By that time, in the very distant future, we too, will be honest enough to admit, modestly, that we "have a long way to go".

CHAPTER TWO

Starting up!

Specialising.
This may seem like a silly question but ask yourself what you *really* want to do? There is no doubt you will prefer some areas of photography to others. Given a choice between industrial, commercial, weddings and babies, public relations, free-lance journalistic photography, aerial, scientific, glamour, fashion, etc. you will have some idea the area which appeals to you most.

But your choice has to tempered with certain considerations. Should you lean towards scientific photography for instance? Unless you intend to work for some in-house set up in a big company, the financial outlay is extremely high and cannot be ignored. Because this is a specialised field you need to know the possible market and, chances are, it will be quite limited. To break into such a specialised vocation needs an outlay in the region of four times greater than that of a general practitioner.

This doesn't mean you can't specialise; far from it! I would recommend it, but only whilst you are earning your bread and butter doing something more-in-demand, or waiting until you have established yourself in some less specialised field.

Further on in this book you will find a 'surprise' chapter on aerial photography. It might come as a surprise to readers, being regarded by some as a definite speciality, but it was included as an example of how, by specialising, you stand to make exceptionally good money. But it has another value.

If nothing else, the chapter will serve as an example of how each and every one of us can become specialist in any field we choose to pursue, given the motivation. Certainly, I feel it is necessary to carve a niche for ourselves in at least one specialist field in our career. It may take time to be regarded as 'expert' in any given domain but, with perseverance and the driving will to improve ourselves and our techniques, it will eventually happen. The rewards are enormous. Not just financially, but as a boost to our confidence. We all need to feel a sense of achievement now and then and, the harder we work towards our chosen goal, the greater the sense of achievement will be.

The first step, of course, is deciding what you wish to succeed in, and that can vary enormously from person to person. Once that decision is made, make it your business to gain as much knowledge on the subject as possible. Read, study, and apply. Searching at every available opportunity for any scrap of information that has been written on the subject and, where possible, we put that knowledge to practical use. Then read some more, all the time expanding yourself and your knowledge, emulating those who have already succeeded.

Within a few months, it is entirely possible to find yourself regarded as a mine of information in your chosen discipline, with practical results improving day by day. Before you know it, you could be breaking new ground, as the learning curve goes off the graph. You're now hooked! Not only that, you are armed: you are authoritative! And yet, less than a year ago, you had no idea what you were capable of, and your inquiring mind continues to expand as knowledge grows. After the newfound euphoria, follows a realisation that the learning curve has somewhat levelled off, and you can look forward to many years of continued improvement.

And so it has been with my pursuit of aerial photography! Read that chapter, and then prove to yourself that the mere reading of it *is* the experience!

Solo Start?

The strange thing about photographers is they usually start off working by themselves, then they will either enter into an established business working for somebody or make some 'partnership' arrangement

After many years, they almost always return to being a solo operator once again.

It may seem to be more secure working with other people but doing so can deny you the huge benefits of being a 'sole proprietor', or even those of forming a Limited Company. I have tried it *all* ways and 'Big' is not necessarily beautiful.

May I suggest you try 'going it alone' first, in your professional career. This way you can start off small and simple with low overheads, gradually building up your equipment as your client base increases. So long as you are not too ambitious and don't immediately commit yourself to the most expensive cameras that exist, or dash out and buy a new car on hire purchase or long-term lease, you should be able to establish yourself within a few months. Remembering that slow growth is less of a strain on your cash-flow than over-committing yourself too soon.

People vary greatly and, when talking about photographers, this is particularly the case. It could be you don't feel ready to take that all-important step of turning freelance or solo professional but, whatever you decide after reading this book, please, always leave your options completely open so that you can change your mind at any time. It can seem hard at first, with so much to consider but, please remember, that is the reason this book was started in the first place – to help would-be professional photographers come to terms with their own special problems.

By way of encouragement may I say this! I make more money, single-handedly, than a previous Company in which I was involved *ever* made with a staff of six, *including* myself as a very busy chief photographer.

Should you contemplate working as a team-member in a joint 'arrangement' with like-minded people, where you share the work and the profits, take care how much money you part with. Most companies have their 'passengers' and it's the genuine workers who carry them. Similarly, if you are in a rowing boat, pulling as hard as you can to cross a wide river and at the opposite end of the boat somebody else is rowing (often in the wrong direction), your journey will be a long and tiring one. The current will probably sweep you all away whilst you battle it out.

The 'Partnership' as an Option.

If you are considering going into partnership with another, think very carefully before doing so. You can always find some very good reasons, at the outset, for joining in a business relationship, but they all tend to be the wrong reasons.

Likely justifications might be, together, you can drum up enough cash necessary to start a business; or, together, you feel you might have a "Jack Spratt and his Wife" arrangement where, perhaps, one is a particularly good photographer, whilst the other has a strength in office management skills. Usually it means one needs the other for any number of reasons, and rarely the right ones. No matter what the initial circumstances, one, or both, parties are most likely to later repent at leisure.

This is not just my opinion, even though it is based upon personal experience. Forming a partnership has to be considered a very risky business and, many times has been compared to choosing a marriage partner.

There are many all-too-obvious similarities. Human nature being what it is, there will be jealousy, arguments and, at the very least, hidden animosities and resentments. Most hinge around finances, shared responsibilities and making decisions. Again, as in marriage, extricating yourself from a doomed relationship could be costly and traumatic. Marriage is the better option, standing a better chance of survival for the simple reason that you sleep together and, hopefully, have a common bond based upon nature's instincts, whereas a business partnership can only be founded upon ego, or the cold, common interest of money.

The possible exception to this rather controversial view is when family members decide to pull together, pooling their resources.

Blood being thicker than water, there are moral bonds and a history of pair-bonding stemming from a childhood together – perhaps even overseen by a father-figure to ensure fair play.

I regularly read the business and financial pages with some philosophical interest and find there are many lessons to be learned from the antics of others. Success stories are always of particular interest to me and I like to know the reason why this, or that, person or Company has succeeded or failed. Few cases are as cut-and-dried as the following one.

A businessman realised the three-cornered partnership he was in was management-heavy and, being fed-up with endless discussions and bickering on Company policy, he decided to 'go it alone'. Using all the resources he had (and no more) he set up a rival business far out of the city where the overheads were low. There, he used his nest egg to purchase the freehold on a warehouse, paying cash, and ran his business on a shoe-string. Gone was his luxury status-symbol car, in its place a Fiat 127 'banger' costing £200. During a period of bad recession he was able to build a successful business following his own four-point rules.

* pay cash wherever you can, don't rely on bankers;
* produce a high-quality product, don't try to compete with the cut-price merchants;
* keep tight control on costs, avoid giving credit wherever possible;
* don't bring in partners, you could waste too much time arguing.

After a couple of years trading, he now finds his pre-tax profits are measured in millions, his warehouse is an investment and an asset and he owns a fleet of seven classic cars, including a Rolls Royce that recently belonged to the Queen. He often pays his suppliers in cash to keep them 'responsive' and, in preparation for his single-market European effort, has bought a chateau in France, tax-allowable, of course!

Now, when he makes a decision, he just goes for it! He alone carries the can, but also reaps the benefits. My case rests.

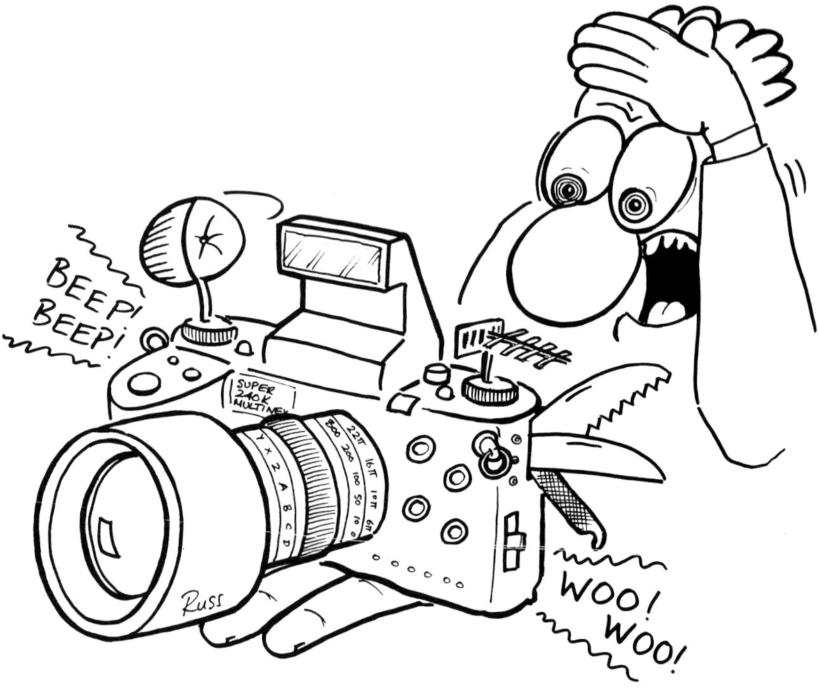

Equipment: the Truth!

Quite honestly, far too much mystique surrounds photography. We meet it all the time and sometimes it seems as though technical barriers are intentionally created by certain individuals to perpetuate this myth. Let us look at these so-called 'technicalities'.

All cameras, regardless of size, are essentially of the same construction. A light-tight compartment or box, with a lens at one end and a means for holding light-sensitive film at the other. To make exposures more controllable, a variable aperture is fitted within the lens and, somewhere between lens and film, a shutter.

The amount of light that falls upon the film is controlled by: a) the size of the aperture selected; b) the length of exposure allowed by the variable shutter under your control.

Some might say this is an over-simplification, but therein lies the problem for many people. It *is* simple. So why should we make it otherwise? Making it hard work is ridiculous, when we are talking *old technology* here. We're in the business of taking photographs and anything we do to make it harder for ourselves can only be counter-productive.

Focussing should never present a problem, even a child is capable of looking through a pair of binoculars, and focussing if necessary. Or, if you are super-lazy, you might have automatic focussing on your camera, leaving only the choosing of the correct exposure combination of aperture and shutter (the biggest single area of "mumbo-jumbo" for most people) and this is solved simply by using a reliable exposure meter.

I'm sure I won't have lost you yet and some of you will be thinking this is rather basic stuff, but I'm simply trying to demonstrate a point! You can take the black magic of photography too far, and become so involved with the technicalities you forget the real objective is to create interesting, well composed pictures.

The camera is a tool; it is your slave, not the other way around. Once you have become familiar with its workings you can forget all techno-fear and concentrate on taking pictures. Never lose sight of the basic simplicity of photography, even if you have an 'all singing and all dancing' camera. Most modern cameras are designed to please the purchaser but the prime objective of some of today's camera manufacturers seems to be to include as many options and gadgets as possible, with endless programs, in an effort to capitalise on the on-board computer's spare kilobytes. There is a place for computers in cameras and I use them myself, but bear in mind you must always be the one in control. If, after missing pictures, you can blame the over-complexity of the controls, then you have definitely *lost* control. The point is proven by looking at cameras the professional chooses. There are less than half a dozen to consider, none of which is totally dependent upon computers, all are solid and rather expensive!

Spending money is one of the easiest things in the world to do and is a most enjoyable pastime. Because there is so much temptation around compelling us to 'invest' in some 'special' piece of equipment, or to up-date a camera simply because the one we are using has been superseded by a later model, we very often succumb. All around us we can justify financial outlay on some pretext or other, but if we surrendered to every desire or tempting offer we would quickly find ourselves in real financial trouble, running the risk of becoming dangerously bogged-down with extra technological learning. Better to fully capitalise on the equipment you already have. There are enough expenses in business without burdening ourselves with hasty spur-of-the-moment extravagances. I can proudly say that the core of my present equipment has lasted me twelve to fifteen years without fault or replacement. The greatest benefit being that I am totally familiar with everything about its workings.

I always try to buy wisely so that my equipment is up to the job and I've always felt comfortable with it and, of course, it still looks workman-like and professional after many years and countless jobs, both on location and in the studio. Those same pieces of equipment still look like new and, more to the point, I am still confident using it.

Some might say it's downright meanness taken to the extreme, considering my earnings. I don't feel miserly, not when I'm laughing, all the way to the bank. There is nothing wrong in sticking to a faithful camera system if it is serving you well, why change for the sake of it? So what if those cameras, lenses, filters and magazine-backs have paid for themselves a hundred times over? Why waste money on a whim?. Yet I've changed my cars every couple of years, to give me peace of mind, for styling reasons and, to some extent to 'look the part'. But you must have noticed that cameras don't physically change all that much. Certainly not professional ones!

Maintenance.

No professional can afford to take his equipment for granted, because if he does, the inevitable will happen. Neglect will catch up with him and he will find himself in the embarrassing situation, probably miles from home, having to cross his fingers and hope everything will be alright and nobody will notice. One solution to reduce this risk is to take certain precautions before the possible event. I recently caused a stir by announcing, via the Mamiya Press Officer, that I had used one camera for twenty years without having it serviced and it had never let me down once! That camera, a Mamiya 645, became newsworthy because it had made a million pounds since its purchase in the early seventies. But, it has never been neglected! I always treat my equipment carefully, as though my livelihood depends on it – and it does!

The camera in question still looks like new because it has never been abused but, inside the magazine-back, there are some signs of wear and, with countless rolls of film still going through it, it's not surprising. But everything works!

I respect it, I keep it clean and away from excess moisture or heat when I can; I don't take it out in a sand-storm and, if it gets wet, I dry it off immediately or at the very first opportunity. I set time aside to give it a 'once over', which consists of a very close inspection of all visible moving parts, looking for excess wear, loose screws and any evidence of swarf. Any specks of dirt or dust are removed with a brush that doesn't 'moult' and if I see any tell-tale sign of metallic swarf around a gear, or any moving part, I take that as a sign of wear which may be indicative of a future trouble spot. Nylon gears are 'the thing' today, and they somewhat reduce this risk-area.

Your relationship with cameras, and other essential photographic equipment, should be something akin to a love affair, and loving-care can come under many guises. I handle my cameras with confidence and firmness. I know every way they can be picked up without risk of dropping them. I am never nervous of causing them damage because I know every curve, every corner, every control. There are rules, of course. Respect and concern for a camera's safety and well-being is paramount. You wouldn't pick up a baby by its ears (even if they did stick out): a market-trader, selling crockery, will toss his plates about as if testing them to destruction to prove how sound they are, but he knows they are not at risk. With our precious cameras, familiarity should never lead us to that sort of contempt or showmanship because it is vital that we show faith in our equipment, and that applies to peripheral equipment too.

If a synchronisation lead has been 'playing up', test it back at the studio with a circuit-tester until the problem is found or throw it away and buy a new one. No! Don't buy one, buy two, of differing lengths perhaps! For the sake of ten pounds, or less, why live with the risk factor when you can make, or lose, hundreds of pounds in a day?

Perhaps a tripod leg has started to stiffen-up and it means you are in danger of not being able to lock it safely in place. Don't ignore it! Far better to dismantle the problem joint to remove this potential source of worry. It probably only needs cleaning and a light smear of Vaseline. Aluminium has a habit of binding on itself, creating an almost-welded joint, without proper maintenance. Far better to spend five minutes removing the worry than looking a complete idiot when your camera crashes to the floor – and so much cheaper!

There are so many things we can do for ourselves, and each little exercise gives us added knowledge and confidence in ourselves and our equipment. There will always be enough to keep us on our toes as progressive photographers, so don't waste valuable time simply surviving each day, breathing a sigh of relief after each assignment. I've said it before, but it's worth saying again, you can't be confident in yourself if you are not confident in your equipment. Keep on top of it, get to know it better than you know the face you shave every day or, if you are female, the face you have learned to make-up so skillfully. Then you can use all your energy doing what you are paid to do. Getting good pictures!

Knowing your camera thoroughly is like having a new, unbelievable freedom, like being reborn. Imagine it! Having no doubts, even in the far reaches of your mind, that the camera will do everything you ask of it. You are the master, knowing every control and every interaction of every control; and it's loaded and ready to go. I can liken it to the feeling of freedom of an Olympic gymnast, who has polished every move to technical perfection and is then free to develop artistic and creative skills. Those magic moments are maybe rare for some people, but they don't have to be!

I think, perhaps, it is the striving for such control and creativity that induces some people to splash-out and buy the most expensive, up-market camera available, but that isn't necessary. Besides, how awful to spend thousands of pounds on a status symbol, only to find your pictures have not improved one iota. Proving something, at least! The 'little guy' who has mastered his second-hand £100 camera will invariably beat the technophile with the latest state-of-the-art machine, and that shouldn't surprise us.

Some of my own best pictures were taken on a folding bellows Zeiss Ikonta before I was twenty-one years old. I knew the lens was good enough to give 'acceptably sharp' results (Novar, not Tessar!), even if it wasn't the best available at the time. The best would have cost me ten times as much, but I had faith in my camera and in my ability to use it, and could therefore simply concentrate on 'seeing' pictures.

If we take time to study and analyse successful pictures, those classics which have stood the test of time and won worldwide acclaim, we will notice that few of them are technically perfect. They are great even though they are not critically sharp. They might be grainy, under-exposed or blurred, or all three! Seldom were they posed, often taken spontaneously, especially those taken in the trenches of World War One. You might say they are great picture because, in bloody war, there is a 'photo-opportunity' second to none, but the photo-journalist still had to release his shutter at the right moment and take the same risks as the fighting troops. A far cry from the world of photography today where so much emphasis is placed on camera-worship, rather than thinking of it as a tool.

So forget this business of switching cameras in an attempt to achieve technical excellence. As with the hi-fi world of sound reproduction, it is a lost cause. You will never be satisfied with what you have because you will always hear, or see, something else that grabs your attention, and so it goes on. With new models coming onto the market, each claiming to be better than its predecessors, you will find yourself not knowing what to believe.

As in all things, you will inevitably end up with a good compromise, with a camera giving a format that caters for your needs and capable of expansion into a good system. This narrows down your choice somewhat, leaving you with an option of probably three manufacturers. Your ultimate choice will be made on feel, looks and price. The quality of lens being taken for granted because you would not have considered 'suspect' outfits in the first place.

Some people don't like to compromise. They demand the very best in everything but, in the real world, we settle for less on practical grounds. When we look at results achieved by ourselves, and others with modest equipment, we sensibly realise that technique is more important than any status symbol. So we end up making the 'sensible' choice. We want reliability, first and foremost, in a camera that is capable of producing sharpish pictures. Getting to know the camera, so that we get the most from it, comes with practice.

What Camera?

Many people believe that to set yourself up as a professional means having a huge selection of equipment, but this is not so, and I will prove it! If I had to choose a single camera for earning money the choice would be simple. It would have to be a medium format camera for the following reasons.

They are eminently versatile, extremely portable and employ an adequately sized format to achieve large reproduction. It is possible to view its transparencies without a projector and most agencies find them totally acceptable. These cameras have a full range of lenses and other accessories and are affordable enough to build a collection. Furthermore, as a kit, it is most impressive to the client. There is also a full range of film available in both 120 or 220 rollfilm and, should you desire it, adaptors for reduced-size formats.

I do own the best 5 × 4 camera in the world (and their 10 × 8 version) but these days it hardly get an airing in the line of work I seem to attract. With medium format I can tackle architecture, aerial, glamour, studio-strobe, portraiture, industrial, advertising, press and social, and much more besides.

When I use 35mm it is generally for the extra convenience of being able to carry the equipment for miles without putting it down. I enjoy that freedom and find I am using it more and more for my own pleasure, rather than for business use. Yes, I still take photographs for pleasure and expect I always shall. I would go so far as to say that my personal interest in photography, for its own sake, has grown even in the past few years.

Exposure Meters.

Having removed all doubts about the role of our cameras and become totally conversant with their use, we are still left with the problem of accurate calculation of exposure, though these days it's not so much a problem as in the past.

What used to be a laborious affair of charts, then extinction meters (now extinct) followed by selenium cells etc, has now progressed to a silicon-celled, battery driven, digital meter accurate to within one tenth of a stop.

Could I really believe such information when previously, it was necessary to bracket exposures to be reasonably sure of success? Accuracy within one tenth of a stop is possibly better than the accuracy of some of my shutters. And no doubt better than the real film speed compared to that indicated by the film manufacturer. In the past few years I have tested these meters in all conditions and they have never yet let me down. I was so impressed I also bought a Minolta Spot Meter for my aerial and long-lens work. Never have things been as easy as they are now. These days, when I collect my films from the lab, I never rush to the light-box. Fear of failing is a thing of the past!

Lighting.

If you have a medium-format camera with a small range of lenses and filters and minor accessories, a reliable exposure meter and sturdy tripod then, with a modicum of lighting, you are well on your way to being adequately equipped for most location work. For 'starters' you could just about manage with one decent flash-gun and a range of brollies, gold, white or silver, and perhaps a translucent one. Naturally, you need an extension cable to extend the flash away from the camera and a meter that can measure ambient light, flash light and combinations of these. Those reliable Minolta Flash Meters will sort out that problem.

The items listed above make up my emergency kit for operating quickly inside offices and factories and I would say more than half my work is no more difficult than that. (I can hear other professionals saying they don't believe it!) The clever bit comes in balancing my flash to daylight (if necessary) and choosing angles, perspective and, occasionally, filters. I frequently bounce my flash (or flashes) off things other than brollies, making use of walls, ceilings, white sheets etc. I work quickly, taking plenty of choices and believe that my strength, as far as my clients are concerned, is in making the most of any situation. Looking beyond 'the obvious' at all times.

To use full studio lighting inside a busy factory is usually quite impossible without stopping the production line, so the technique described above was improvised out of necessity. This is often the secret of good pictures in difficult circumstances. Improvisation!

Back-up Cameras.
I believe in back-up cameras, or at least an extra camera body. Quite often I find myself a long way from home on an important assignment, or I might be doing a day's aerial photography, and the peace of mind it gives me is well worth it. There's never been an occasion when I've needed the back-up, but to have two camera bodies loaded can be a great advantage when you are busy.

Equipment and Studio Hire.
In your early days in professional photography you could find yourself in the position where you are asked to do something you cannot tackle with your existing equipment. Even seasoned veterans meet this problem and because this is a common predicament there

are quite a few photographic suppliers who rent out gear, specialised or otherwise. The revenue from your job ought to cover the hire charges easily. The invoice for the hire can be put through your books, just like any other work-related expense. Later, when you have built up your earnings, you can buy what you need, but there will always be some items you cannot really justify buying.

Likewise, if a client wants you to photograph something in the studio and you don't even have one yet or, if you do, it's far too small, again this is something you can hire, by the day or part-day. Better still, even though you may be working independently, you might have a photographer-acquaintance who is benevolent enough to help you out. Another photographer might need *your* help one day so don't be surprised if you find fellow-professionals very helpful!

To console the purists amongst you, I am still called upon to tackle location work requiring enough lighting equipment to fill a Range Rover but, unless I'm specifically asked to 'put on a show' for the client's benefit, I realistically concentrate on technique to give me repeat orders. I try to give 'value for money', and you can't do that if most of your time is spent lugging gear around from one location to the next. My customers appreciate my style, and *do* keep coming back!

NOTES

CHAPTER THREE

Increased Sales and Self-Promotion.

Where Do New Clients Come From?
This, to many aspiring photographers, is perhaps the biggest single worry. If there were guarantees of a good solid core of regular clients who paid well, there would be no problem. Our would-be photographer would simply hand in his notice at the factory, pick up his potted plant and walk out of the office, or come off 'the dole', immediately.

Many would-be professionals may already suspect they have the necessary expertise to embark upon photography as a career, but are apprehensive about 'getting started'. They realise that, to survive, they need work and, without contacts or a small core of potential clients, they are lost in the wilderness.

Portfolio.
If you are considering turning professional it's likely you have had a camera for some time and, consequently, will already have a selection of photographs to show for it. Most of those pictures are probably of a personal, rather than a commercial, nature and unsuitable for self-promotional purposes.

To persuade a potential customer that you are capable of doing something useful for him, your 'portfolio' should include examples relating to his particular field. This may mean taking some photographs specifically aimed at that market. For instance, if you are motivated towards architectural photography then you will obviously need pictures showing fine buildings. The architect is unlikely to be impressed by 'baby' pictures, or by a beautiful 'bride and 'groom' shot of which you are particularly proud. Likewise, if you wish to break into the advertising field, doing 'pack-shots' for instance, you would probably need to take a few shots specially for your portfolio. Most households contain numerous suitable items and almost any new-looking product would do. Clocks, ornaments, Sony Walkman and many boxed items are suitable, or even some of your own photographic gear, such as a camera. You might even approach a local Company for products to practice on, repaying them with a few free prints. Who knows, they might then engage you on a regular basis, as a paying customer. Whatever your particular leaning, it is most important for you to be motivated towards that subject for you to excel.

Half a dozen good examples of your work should be sufficient for each client. Go for quality rather than quantity, because you may be judged by your worst picture, not your best. Don't be in too big a hurry to rush off to 'flash' the photographs at the prospective client, obtain a second opinion from somebody whose judgment you value – and take heed of what is said. *Your* favourite picture might be cherished for some personal reason but the one that was easiest to achieve could be the best, from an entirely objective point of view. This exercise has to be on-going throughout your career, so make a study of what is 'in vogue' and don't forget to polish up your presentation.

Local Press.

Do you believe in advertising? Many of your prospective clients do and, therefore, you know where to find them, particularly in the business pages of local newspapers.

We're looking at 'picking' the local press, gathering a file on local businesses that you would like to service, finding out all you can about local industry and commerce. Decide what you can already do, or perhaps would like to do, and select your prospective clients to suit. If you hate machine-tools, or simply can't do that sort of work because you haven't yet got the right equipment or expertise, then concentrate on what motivates you and what you are able to do, bearing in mind your resources. In my career I have found myself specialising in a subject that has started to bore me, or perhaps isn't as lucrative as another sphere. That is the time for change, because we all work better when happy in our work.

Advertising.
Anyone can advertise in their local newspaper or in any journal. It's just a question of writing some 'copy' and paying the advertising fees, which are never cheap. For an advert to be successful it has to recoup more than the cost of the insertion. The best forms of advertising are frequently the cheapest so do not discount the local 'free' newspapers which survive on thousands of classified ads every week. The 'trick' is to persuade a layout designer friend to compose something that really catches the eye and to place it where it will do the most good. Quite often the price quoted for placing such adverts is negotiable, so be prepared to haggle to some extent.

If you took up every offer from tele-sales people to advertise in their particular journal, you wouldn't survive for a year; they would bankrupt you. You must be selective or you might as well stand in a shower tearing up five pound notes. It is generally thought that the best value-for-money is obtained through your local Yellow Pages, but maybe in your first year you would have to give this a miss because a year in Yellow Pages costs about the same as a very good 35mm camera. Most people get more than their money back by advertising in this way and it has other benefits too. Some will judge your credibility on the size and style of your advert on the assumption that, if you are serious enough to splash out on Yellow Pages, you are not one of those 'here today, gone tomorrow' cowboys. 'Talking Pages', a relatively new concept, could prove fruitful, and you can change the 'content' of their spiel at short notice.

One-to-One Selling.
When a would-be client first contacts you, and that is usually by telephone, he has probably never had dealings with you and even though he may have come to you on the recommendation of a third party, he is making a cold-call. (In sales jargon that means a first contact, often out of the blue, and without warning or preliminaries). However, in this case he is buying and not selling. He has to decide whether or not you are up to the job, whether your prices are reasonable and, most important (and not to be taken too lightly) whether he likes you or not. He assumes, if you are professional, you know what you are doing with a camera, but he (or she), will be

trying to decide whether you have the expertise to do the kind of job he requires.

He knows that a professional photographer who is an expert at photographing babies, and does nothing else, could be floundering doing close-up photography of pieces of broken machinery, or the pouring of white-hot metal in a foundry. In making his decision, he has to hold a conversation with you and, in return, get some feed-back. He is unlikely to ask, "Are you good at taking photographs of white-hot metal?", or "Have you had experience in metallurgy?" But this is what he has to determine. This potential client might possibly become a major source of revenue for you one day, spending £1000 per month or more, so you must appear capable and confident. Don't go over the top boring him with your exploits and daring-do, plunging into a tirade of past successes and generally having an ego trip. He wants to assess your abilities, so quiet confidence is the better approach.

Assure him, by all means, that solving his problems is your stock-in-trade. Suffice to say, you are quite familiar with his subject and can convince him with a few well chosen words. Being able to converse in many topics is definitely an advantage in our line of work. Again, don't get too excited and overdo it, you could get into deep water on a subject the client surely knows more about. Assurance is the keyword and your motivation. He will be more likely to look upon you favourably if you appear genuinely interested in his subject. He knows people work better if they are genuinely absorbed by what they are doing so, confi-dence without boasting is the rule. Assurance in your familiarity with his problem and keenness without begging. You will know when you have accomplished this exercise in human relations, and so will he. You will win some and lose some, but you will learn by your early mistakes if you want to succeed. And don't regard lack of success as failure, but merely a temporary set-back to be added to your growing experience.

Sometimes apparent success in this type of selling will cause a photographer to make the mistake of appearing over-confident.

Some clients can suffer that in a man, others immediately raise their barriers and decide to try elsewhere, hoping to find a more modest individual who is not a know-all (though possibly less able). In all things, moderation is the keyword. Until you know your client better, it is wise to treat him with the same respect you might afford your doctor. Good manners not only cost nothing, but could make you plenty. It's like attending an interview for a job really, and that is exactly what it is, except over the 'phone you don't have the benefit of eye-to-eye contact, making the dialogue that much more important.

You might like to try telephone sales yourself, ringing round to see if anyone could use your help. If you have the expertise, then why not exercise it! The cost of a 'phone call is much less than that of a advert in the local press, but there is an acquired technique that takes some mastering, and you have to get used to the occasional rebuff. Choose a time when you are feeling positive in yourself and, if it doesn't seem to be going too well, simply shrug your shoulders and try again another day!

It's a well known fact that selling yourself, either over the 'phone or in person, is much harder psychologically when you are worried, or desperate. Like facing a big dog who can smell fear, you feel vulnerable, and that is not good for your morale, or for your confidence.

Your aura is wrong, if you like. Your body language changes when you are down, and it might just show.

Whether it is you making the calls or you answering enquiries from interested parties, using the same chat technique every time not only gets boring, but may not necessarily work so well as when you vary it. Adjust your style of approach as you 'read' each situation, taking your cue from the would-be client. You don't have to entertain him, although I know somebody who uses that method very well, someone who has that special gift of charm with a natural sense of humour. Until you have gained some success in this field of telephone sales, it is better to be yourself. You *may* have 'the knack' of course, the ability to succeed in conversation, but it is a part of life that can only improve with practice.

Don't expect everybody to like you, as I did many years ago. If that is what you expect then you haven't taken human nature into account. To discover somebody has taken an immediate dislike to you, for no apparent reason, can be a dreadful blow to one's ego. Accept that nobody is perfect, including yourself, and enrol in life's school of diplomacy and good human relations. The rewards are enormous, not only in business but in every aspect of life.

Techniques to attain in one-to-one selling;

* practice on 'minor' contacts
* emanate professionalism
* be enthusiastic without gushing;
* be respectful and diplomatic;
* be confident, without boasting;
* be conversant with as many subjects as possible;
* remember, you can't win them all;
* and accept the possibility of failure as a necessary step towards eventual success.

Self-promotion.
Don't wait for the World to beat a path to your door, it might never happen. As photographers we are media-men, and should use some of those associated media-skills to further our own business. It's a strange fact that although photographers spend much of their working lives assisting others in their promotions, they seldom lend those talents to their own cause. Yet we are in an ideal position to make things 'happen'!

I would like to give you an example. This book was born to fill a real need by students. It's writing was made possible because I had been a professional photographer all my life and, consequently, knew many of the answers. I already had a word-processor to help me with the task and had the urge to plough something back into the profession in return for what I had received from photography. Then I needed a little help from my friends!

The contacts made in professional photography are many and various. I knew something of the printing and publishing world, having worked with advertisers, layout artists and publicity people, and knew about market research and distribution; even packaging and paperwork. In fact, everything to *make* it happen was already at my fingertips.

And so it is with you, because the people who are your associates in business are the very people to help you promote yourself. It would be foolish not to capitalise on that fact.

Although you, and your results, are your best advertisement, and word-of-mouth recommendation is the best way to expand your existing business, you have at your disposal many alternatives. There are ways in which you can improve your visible image and sales using tried and tested promotional techniques.

When sending out 'mailshots' (letters to prospective clients stating your services), you could include a photographic example of your work which is worthy of putting on their office wall – with your name prominently on show, of course. People are loathe to throw away real photographs, so you stand a good chance of making an impact. The subject of your free photograph is up to you but it has to be chosen carefully, bearing in mind it has to have general appeal.

Costing more to produce, but more effective, would be a colour poster containing your best work to serve as a permanent reminder to everybody that you exist. Some people use calendars, diaries, pens, key-fobs and the like, to put their name forward and stay in the limelight. Such items can accompany mailshots, be presents at Christmas time, or represent something to leave with a prospective client when you call on him.

Taking a leaf out of the designer and agency book, there are manuals produced that are a folio for leading media-men and their work, and some high-flying photographers subscribe to this useful, but rather expensive, form of self-promotion. Also, those same people use independent agents whose task it is to travel the country promoting the services of media people who pay them on a 'commission' basis.

How Others See Us!

At various points in this book it is inevitable that I give my own opinion, albeit based upon long, and sometimes painful, experience. To reinforce and verify that opinion I have taken the trouble to do some market-research to check out my facts from time to time, expanding my thoughts on any particular subject.

Whilst musing over the topic of what might motivate an art director, or a designer, to enlist a particular photographer for an assignment, I decided to make a couple of 'phone calls to check out my own theories. It was reassuring to find that there were no surprises as far as my own beliefs were concerned, but I noticed that some art directors did have some quite strong feelings in certain areas. My full findings follow.

Every art director, account executive or designer has got a choice of several photographers he can call upon, on a 'horses for courses' basis. The photographer he appoints for a particular assignment is chosen for the qualities he is reputed to have. It goes without saying that each photographer on this man's books will be capable of delivering sharp, well composed, imaginative and correctly exposed pictures. The final decision is made according to the individual skills of each photographer.

For instance, if it's a small job, involving only studio table-top photography, he will choose the operator who has proved himself in that area before. If it's only one or two creative shots, to be delivered on 5 × 4 transparency, he knows the right man would be somebody who consistently surprises him with his visual ingenuity. For a long drawn-out assignment, involving lots of travelling, when the photographer has to work on his own initiative, he would choose somebody with staying-power who is also conscientious and always 'delivers the goods'.

Sometimes, where a tight budget is essential, the decision is a compromise between the cheapest and the best, or he may negotiate a lower price from his first or second choice.
No surprises so far!

Often, a photographer is chosen because he gets along with precocious children, for his charm and personality, for his ability to handle awkward customers or is one who doesn't mind taking the 'flak' from a rude and difficult client. But there are other non-photographic reasons to influence our ad-man's decision.

It all comes down to how we, as photographers, are perceived by others, and that was the bit that surprised me!

Apparently, we photographers are a strange, twitchy lot (I knew that bit!). We all have our qualities, but we can be difficult too! Some of our lesser qualities include: temperamental, over-the-top, too humble, too arrogant, too wimpish and meek, too forceful or just downright rude! I guess I'm in there somewhere.

I've always believed the way to get the best results, for director and client alike, is to work closely within the director's brief and, when I wanted to 'do my own thing', to give *that* as an extra bonus. And, presumably, this is the right way! But there are a few of us who, regardless of our directive, accept a brief then insist on giving the ad-man a 'fait accompli'. This they don't like!

Something I have difficulty coming to terms with is the fact that some directors resent photographers assuming they are *equal* to themselves, in the 'pecking order', that is! Some designers see themselves as the boss (which they are) and they like it to stay that way. I guess the best solution is to recognise the problem of 'pecking order' and, so long as the photographer can still find his motivation, there should be no problem! Personally speaking, total humility is not my strong suit.

It's just as well to know these things.

Reciprocal Arrangements.

There is a lot to be said for cementing good relations with designers and advertising people, and there can be quite a few opportunities to help each other gain business. As photographers, we are often 'at the sharp end' when it comes to receiving enquiries. Imagine this scenario! A businessman who needs a photographer finds your name in the Yellow Pages. He telephones you to fix an appointment for you to call on him, whereupon you quickly observe that it is not just a photographer he needs, but a much wider service. He does need a photographer, but he also requires some publicity in the form of a leaflet or brochure, supported by your pictures of course. He knows of no brochure experts, or graphic designers so, as you know plenty of them, you are in a position to recommend who you think best suited for the job. You can discuss it with the client and decide whether he waits for a call from one of your 'associates' or, perhaps, rings them himself. Either way, you have created work for the designer who, in turn, returns the compliment by recommending you to one of *his* contacts. This 'back scratching' can go on indefinitely and all helps keep the wheels turning and the wolf from the door. So you see, you can be "more than just a photographer".

Surviving the Winter.

When photographers look back over a typical year, to analyse monthly turnover, they invariably notice there are busy periods and quiet spells. The hectic months support the not-so-busy ones, and they tend to shrug their shoulders and say that it's the same for all businesses, and always will be.

They may even console themselves by reasoning that they have survived thus far in the marketplace, accepting the ups and downs, so why shouldn't they survive forever? The keyword is "survive". They may survive, but will they flourish? They could go on this way forever, simply grateful to be in work and giving a good service, and proud to have survived at all. This is a common enough problem for many businesses, but there is something positive that can be done and anything is better than accepting the status quo.

It is obviously wiser to try to stabilise fluctuating turnover to some degree, so you remove the deepest troughs first. If your worst turnover month is January, maybe some special promotional offers would rectify the position. Perhaps you could increase your output by some 50 percent simply by ringing round your regular clients to wake them up after their two or three weeks Seasonal Holiday. After the Christmas/ New Year break, you have the excuse of wishing them a "Happy New Year", and what better time to socialise and chat a little? If that doesn't work maybe you should use the 'flat spot' to your advantage, and catch up on all those chores you've been putting off, or maybe decide to take your holidays somewhere exotic during our long, dark days of Winter, taking your camera, of course!

Go where the Money is!

When looking for new business, there's more to selecting your clients than simply sticking a pin in a business newspaper; it's an art, but one that can be mastered. If you could always choose your customers then, if you thought about it, you would sensibly go for the ones who are doing best in the market-place. These are the ones most likely to have money to spare for advertising and promotion. You might think that a financially successful Company would have no need to promote themselves, but there are several reasons why they would, and should do so.

A Company that's having a particularly good time, is likely to be in a position where they would want to consolidate their image in the face of their competition. This could be done by producing an expensive glossy brochure, or by staging a lavish exhibition. Both options need photography! Furthermore, if their profits have been very high, it would be of added advantage for them to spend money on tax-allowable promotions of various sorts before the end of their tax-year. *Somebody* will be engaged to do it for them, so why not you! Go where the money is! Why struggle along with customers who are themselves struggling along?

When the 'property' market is booming, and interest rates are low, go for the property developers. Always go for the top of the tree. Builders may make thousands, but commercial property developers make millions and, likewise, spend more on promotion and image-building too!

In times of recession encourage those who actually benefit from such hard times because there are always those that do. I know people who became rich because of the last World War, dealing in the millions of tons of scrap left over after the event. They made millions! When things are nationally bad be ready, in advance, to capitalise on the poor beggars who have to liquidate their assets. Woo the machine tool auctioneers! One man's bad fortune is another man's providence! Be realistic and accept that if *you* don't do it, somebody else will and, if you make a specially good job of it, your efforts will raise many thousands of pounds extra revenue for the unfortunate liquidating Company.

Build a broad base of successful clients, but always review the current situation on a regular basis, watching the financial newspapers like a hawk!

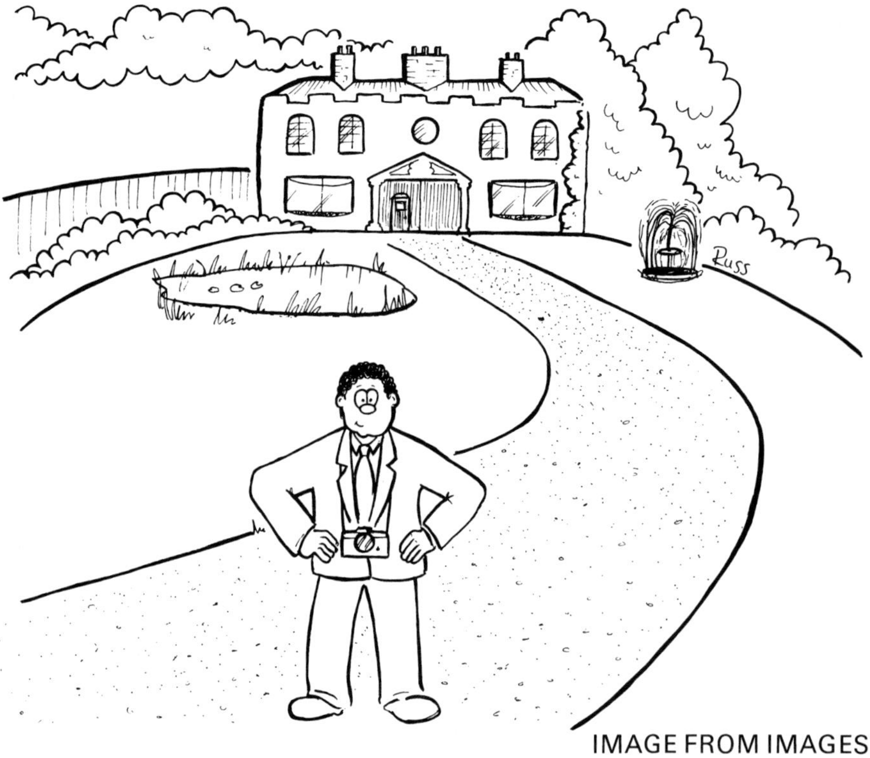

IMAGE FROM IMAGES?

CHAPTER FOUR

Choosing...and Losing your Clients. (or you win some – you lose some!)

When things go quiet.
Why are the customers so quiet? Why doesn't the 'phone ring? Dare you ring them to see if they are still alive? If this carries on you will be eating stale bread next month. But you like cake! So what do you do? You may have a hard core of, say, six regular clients and anything up to a dozen occasional ones and last month you didn't know which way to turn, you were so busy. Now it's as if the word has got around that you have leprosy. Or worse....perhaps they all think you're a useless photographer! Why?

Self doubt begins to creep in and, whilst last month at this point you were looking forward to a rest, now you've got it you don't like it! Even the busiest and most successful studios have times when things 'go quiet'. It can come about for several reasons and, although it can usually be avoided, we should not lose heart. Let us first of all consider why this phenomenon occurs.

There are, for instance, some periods when the National economy is severely deflated, causing financial hardship amongst businesses generally. This eventuality is covered in the chapter on Increased Sales and Self-Promotion, and requires special tactics. Another cause may be that one of your customers has prematurely exceeded their annual sales budget, leaving nothing 'in the pot' for further spending on photography. A reason, also out your control, could be mis-management within your client's sales force. Workers Unions traditionally blame the management for poor trading figures, but it is often true. A certain worldwide machine-tool manufacturer 'bit the dust' a short while ago because they acted too late to prevent the Japanese competition from 'stealing' their market. Too little, too late was the undoing of that giant and so thousands of supporting industries suffered in the 'domino effect'.

Fortunately such catastrophes are quite rare. Neglect on our own part is a more likely cause. We can be blithely sailing along, doing quite nicely for perhaps some eighteen months when, suddenly, we realise that work has stopped coming in. Analysing our customer base, we notice that the sector of the market we have been so busy servicing are all in a similar line of business which has suffered a slump. Putting your eggs in one, or even two baskets is a risky thing to do because, should that market dry-up for any reason, you will be left high and dry. Motto: look after your old clients, even when you are 'rolling in it' working for rich new ones. Nothing lasts for ever, as I keep saying!.

Now for some home truths and the main reasons for the demise of most photographers' clientele.

Having done my homework, and considerable market research, I have to declare that the major factors causing clients to go to pastures new are rudeness, inefficiency, and a couldn't-care-less attitude on the part of photographer or staff. If this is true of any photographer, perhaps he should reappraise his situation, changing his image or the photographic field in which he is working! Or fall by the wayside.

The Medicine.

Whatever has been done to upset a client can be undone, eventually. But, in the meantime, we should learn from the experience to prevent it happening again!

First of all, let's look at what you should have done – last month, and the month before. Love, and business, is like a comfortable pair of shoes, both should be kept in a state of good repair but, when you feel comfortable, you tend to wear them 'into the ground'. Your business, your loving partner and your comfortable shoes, need some caring attention from time to time because, without it, they fall into neglect. With regular attention they will serve you well for a lifetime, I have shoes that are twenty-five years old.

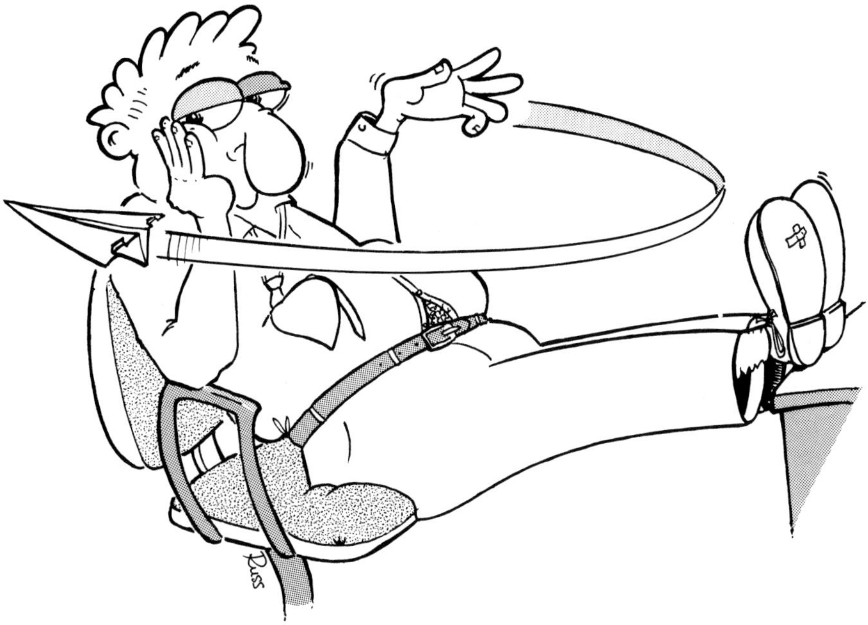

So what should you have done to avoid your present dilemma? For a start, when you were busy last month, some clients rang when you were out on location. Was there anybody in to take a message? If not, do you have an answerphone? Either way let's assume you did get the messages. Did you ring back? Or were you too busy? That's bad! It is also insulting. Your biggest strength is that you *care* about your clients. You could lie about the message not being passed on but, not only is that dishonest, it smacks of inefficiency. You may not immediately think that someone else's incompetence reflects badly upon you, but I'm afraid it does if that person works with you, or for you. Think about it. If you are in the habit of telling lies, no matter how 'white' or justified you think they are, you will be found out eventually. Some of my clients tell some whoppers and I usually know, but it doesn't hurt me too much. For some, lying is part of their life and their character, but not everybody is as philosophical about such things as I am.

Alright. As far as you know there were no messages and, if there had been, you would have rung back. So what else? Do you always give your client the best attention? They ring you for all sorts of reasons, not just to book your time for a few hours. If they ring to order a couple of prints just as you're going out on a big job, do you react as if it's too much trouble to make up the chemicals? You know, by the time you have driven 100 miles, done a few hours photography and driven back, it will be late evening. Yet he wants his prints first thing in the morning! You could say, "No, I'm too busy"?. If you do, he'll look elsewhere and you'll probably never see him again. He's worth about £1000 per year to you now, perhaps treble that next year. He has a reputation for being something big in the Round Table, or is a Mason. In short, he has connections. Can you really afford to let him down? To upset him? The answer is simply "No!" But even if he wasn't well connected and a handy bloke to be 'in with', you must accept the rough with the smooth. It's putting yourself out for people that impresses them most. So, when someone asks for a couple of prints worth a profit of a mere few pounds, as you are about to depart to earn two or three hundred, why not say you've got to go to Timbuctoo but when you get back you'll certainly do the prints, assuring the client they will be on his desk first thing the next morning! That is caring, and it shows. Much better than saying you're going fishing and, if you get back before tea, you'll try to find time to do his prints but you can't promise! Clients expect you to care enough to put yourself out, even though you would rather be in the pub.

Photography may be a profession but it is also a service industry, whether you like it or not.

Wandering Clients.

There are a dozen reasons why a client might go elsewhere. Sometimes it's in their nature to 'hop about', trying this photographer, then that one. Or it may be that they're financially insecure and move around when they have run out of credit. Maybe there has been a change of staff in their sales/ publicity department and the new man has his own 'pet' photographer. Sometimes a business takeover can rock the boat for you. Occasionally a Company will form its own 'in-plant' photographic department.

Or, horror of horrors, you might have let the client down. Sometimes only once is enough for them to look for another photographer. Don't distress yourself, or take it too personally, it happens to us all at sooner or later!

It can sometimes be difficult keeping up with your workload and you may find yourself standing-by for good weather for one client, but have an interior assignment to do for another. What do you do? Obviously a decision has to be made and, as the weather forecast is not good, you keep your 'interior' appointment. No sooner have you set up your lights, your 'yuppie' 'phone rings. The client cheerfully informs you that the weather is perfect at his end, and asks, "Where are you?"

You tell him, and he is not pleased. He explains that unless you can come straight over he will have to make other arrangements. You now have a conflict of interests between two very good clients. Decision time yet *again*. You will probably choose the job you've already started, letting the other client get fixed up elsewhere and you may not hear from him for perhaps a year. You think you have lost him forever but, eventually, he will remember how good you are, compared to the photographer who helped him out of a spot that time. You've had your wrists slapped, metaphorically speaking, and the client silently vows to make firmer arrangements in future.

Sometimes you won't find out why a customer has ceased to use you until you read about him in the liquidation/ insolvency columns. If he had used your services in the previous three months you *might* have been caught out for several hundred pounds, so you count your blessings!

Cost is seldom the real reason for losing a client, unless your fees are really excessive for what you have to offer. You should always be able to justify your charges, even though you know others might be cheaper. The best justification for your prices is giving value for money, not forgetting your own motivation and loyalty. With regular clients there is a constant personal contact, so this problem is easily monitored. The once or twice-a-year client is the hardest to tie down but, in reality, it is these people who need nurturing so they grow to become once or twice-a-month people.

There are too many reasons to list here why a client shifts his allegiance, suffice to say that it is an ongoing situation and all we can do is look after our customers to the best of our abilities. The rest is usually just human nature.

On the 'Plus' Side.

There is one element you should be aware of which, in some way, is a consolation for losing a client: nothing is forever, in business or in life. So often as one door closes, another opens. I successfully serviced one particular client for some twenty-five years and had started to think that it would go on eternally but they fell upon hard times and eventually used one of their staff to take 'snaps' instead of employing me. I was quite shocked, after so many years of faithful service, but had to be philosophical about it, grateful for what I had already received.

But there was a 'plus' side to it all. During those long years in which they had been my bread-and-butter client, I had practically organised my whole life around them. Lately their work had entailed an hour or two here, an hour there, chopping my working day about horrendously. When it all stopped, I suddenly found myself busy and more available in other directions, working full-days instead of part-days. My turnover almost doubled overnight, simply because I had lost a client!

Choosing Your Clients.

Yes, you are very much in control when it comes to whom you work for, and the type of work that you do. If you find yourself getting 'browned off' with a certain customer and their demands then, frankly, you must end up blaming yourself if you are totally honest. When you work for yourself, you are your own task-master – it took me all of twenty-five years to learn that! I don't know why because it seems so obvious now.

However, I console myself that hard-learned lessons are the ones that sink in deepest, and along the way a wealth of experience is gained. I have found that even the most painful and unpleasant happenings in life have some value at a later date, though some are avoidable and have come about by taking a wrong route, or by making an error of judgment.

Philosophy aside, let us look at the title of this section again. If you are working as an employee then the type of work you are expected to do is probably mapped out for you, particularly if you are working for a large company as an in-plant photographer. The best way to control this is by adopting a particular style, approach, or method of working that appeals to you. I am, of course, assuming that you are in charge of your own destiny, or expecting to be soon, and are in a position to make some major policy decisions concerning your future and your work. Because if that is the case, please assume the proper attitude and remember that the buck stops with you.

As a beginner, *or* as a seasoned veteran, you might be tempted to take on all the work that is put your way, particularly if the coffers are low or things are relatively quiet – we are all prone to that. We might, for example, find ourselves sweating in a noisy, smelly, factory environment on a very hot day and hating every minute of it. If that sort of work is not to your liking then, having done it once, you could vow never to do it again. If it pays very well, and the pain is worth it, then "put up and shut up" whilst doing it. Look forward to a better day in the not-too-distant future when you can simply inform your client that you are now specialising in calendar work, holiday brochures, or maybe going off to Detroit City to compile a photographic study of pre-1930 cast-iron drain covers. What I am saying is, if you are truly your own master, you ought to be doing what you really want to do.

In practice, of course, we all end up doing certain jobs we regret having taken on but, so long as they don't take over our lives completely and we still have a good proportion of inspiring and financially rewarding work, it's not so bad. We naturally give our 'all' to the boring and undesirable work and can even become quite involved with it if we make the effort. The danger is that we can become trapped by our self-imposed chores. We then have a commitment to the client, and eventually to ourselves with our over exaggerated sense of responsibility.

The longer this is allowed to continue, the harder it will become to break the habit. As soon as personalities come into it and we develop a loyalty to the client, we could end up treating the work as a bread-and-butter job and simply fall into a 'routine of acceptance'. This is the best reason for being firm at the outset. As soon as you can, decide the direction in which you want to go and, if you are not sure, let experience decide for you, but don't allow yourself to get trapped on a treadmill.

The world is full of people who have spent a whole lifetime in a job they have simply tolerated. Some have even given up dreaming totally, accepting their 'lot'. If it pays the mortgage and keeps the wolf from the door, why change now, they think. They will shrug their shoulders and console themselves that things could have been worse, or that they did it for the kids' sake, in some martyr-like way. If life on Earth is *not* a rehearsal for a second re-run at some later date, then why waste it?

Life should be about achievement. Gradually building up a store of learning from the nursery, from our parents and teachers, and from life's experiences generally. We become influenced, to a large extent, by people we meet along the way, family, friends, what we read, see and hear. Sometimes we are left to our own devices having no one to guide us, but don't become an 'island', kidding yourself you prefer it that way!

If, having had a smattering of 'general practice', you feel you have had enough experience to gauge the direction in which you would prefer your career to go, finally ask yourself this (and forgive me if I mention money). Have a specialist subject if you like, so long as you are personally motivated enough to pursue it, but have you chosen an area where you can expect to have continuing work, and where there is a demand? And, most important of all, an area with a good number of wealthy clients willing to pay the going rate for your services? You will then, with perseverance, soon become most proficient in your chosen field because we all learn quickest doing what we want to do.

With such specialised experience and knowledge we can command a respectable and professional fee. Learn the going rate and keep yourself informed of all price increases or, in a couple of years, you could find your fees forty or fifty percent lower than anybody else's. Bad business indeed. If you are cheaper than anyone else, apart from you suffering financially, it might be suspected that it reflects your ability. If your prices are higher than anybody else's you will either be told so by a client, or notice that customers cease to employ you because you may not be giving value for money. The temptation to reduce your fees simply because ill-informed prospective clients think they are too high, is always there. If you are tempted to do this too often you will be inviting trouble. Remember, there will always be somebody who can undercut your fees. Unless you are really keen to do a particular job, don't get caught up in haggling. Far better to be working a thirty-hour week for a good return than a fifty-hour week for the same amount. Who wants to be a busy fool?

Your daily rate, based on an eight hour day, will seem horrendously high to those who are ignorant of the going rate, but perfectly acceptable to those who know better. So long as you continue to maintain professional results, you are perfectly justified in charging professional prices.

So you can see that you have control over some less desirable customers by rationing them on price alone. You don't refuse to work for them, simply price yourself out of their market. Besides, those who haggle at the onset of a job are more likely to haggle when your invoice arrives on their desk, and this is to be avoided. You will find that true professionals are fully aware of the professional rate in your field.

Filling your time.

Most businesses have a peak period during their trading year which can be foreseen by looking at previous years and, likewise, the quiet spells are predictable in the same way.

Taking wedding photographers as a rather obvious example, we see forward-looking businesses launch promotional portraiture or baby photography during the leaner Winter months, and they might also take on some commercial work between weddings, during the week, so as to create a steady flow of productivity. This naturally keeps them from getting bored, or even depressed, and gives a general feeling of job satisfaction whilst simultaneously topping up their bank balance.

If you are anticipating, for whatever reason, a lull in business during the next few months, plans ought to be made in advance to fill your time effectively.

If, having taken the plunge into professional photography, you have days when you can say you have nothing to do, then quite honestly I won't believe you! There is always something waiting to be done in our job and your eventual success will depend on it! If you doubt it, run your eyes down the following typical list of chores that constantly need attention.

* review price lists;
* catch up on paperwork/ letter writing;
* invoicing/ chase debtors;
* read recent journals/ self-improvement;
* check over any 'suspect' equipment;
* improve studio facilities;
* catch up on 'phone calls/ try telephone-sales;
* 'sus' out new locations for models;
* study the opposition, particularly the successful;

* rectify your 'image', if necessary, or polish it;
* concentrate on creative self-work/ photo-library;
* polish new photographic techniques;
* take in an exhibition to keep up enthusiasm and morale;
* diversify to new fields, if necessary;
* buy new equipment, and acquaint yourself with it;
* order film/ paper stocks;
* do bank reconciliation, or count your money.

Quite honestly, this list could go on to fill many pages, so there never *will* be times when there is nothing to do. The problem will likely be how to drag yourself away for relaxation, which we all have to do now and then!

You might try this trick in your spare time.
You may have heard the saying, "You are what you think you are!" It's to do with self-image and is one of the 'Natural Laws' which, when employed, can do wonders for you and your business. Briefly, it means how you, and your abilities, are perceived by others is determined by your own self-image, by the way you have programmed your brain.

Tell yourself you hate paper-work, and you certainly will.
If you are convinced you are a clumsy operator, it is likely the way you will be. The cure is to re-program your beliefs, replacing all negative thoughts with only positive ones. It works! So, be careful what you set your heart on, for you will surely get it!

NOTES

CHAPTER FIVE

Getting Organised.

For those who have the energy and inclination, it is almost unbelievable how much can be fitted into a week, but we will look at just one day. Each day should be planned, if possible, and the best time to do it is a couple of minutes during the previous evening when your mind still clearly holds the activities of the present day. Make a list of 'chores' or tasks you must tackle during the next day. Assuming, of course, it is not one of those days when you are up at dawn (or earlier) and driving a couple of hundred miles for a day-long booking, and then travelling back. I've always been a great believer in lists, not for their own sakes, but as an aid to getting organised. Although the human brain is a marvellous thing, it needs a little help from time to time. There's a tremendous amount of stored information, and many ideas, in our heads but, just like our desk-top computers, unless we organise the information that it holds, we can't always gain access to it. Now and then we have to take the initiative to organise ourselves and writing things down is a good way of doing it. At the end of the day, or at the very beginning of one, it is a good idea to make a list of things you plan to do today, tomorrow, or at sometime in the future. You will soon discover whether your brain prefers late or early. Either way, simply jot down a list, in any order as it comes to you, of pressing jobs or outstanding chores. There will be a mixture of personal and business memory-joggers which could go something like this;

* RETURN TELEPHONE CALL from Alan Brown, (major client, and most important);
* NUMBER NEGATIVES from yesterday's job, and put in-hand;
* GO TO BANK to put in £2000 cheque (from yesterday's post, but you were out all day earning more money);
* ORDER EXTRA FILM for next week's big job;

* TRY TO think of excuse to RING TONY, (most recently acquired client) to prompt his brain into thinking photography; don't be a nuisance by 'bending his ear', take your cue from him;
* buy some ENVELOPES, and whilst in town get
* BIRTHDAY PRESENT for Sue;
* HAIRCUT;
* go to COLOUR LAB to collect work, take other work;
* make time to CHECK CAR, oil and water, before long trip at end of week.

Some days the list goes on and on and it has all been stored in your head. Putting it onto paper allows you to see what needs to be done and, as other ideas and problems occur, you add them to the list, crossing off those you have done. Naturally, there will be a correct order in which to tackle your chores but the very act of committing your thoughts to paper helps in itself. It clears away that nagging, worried feeling that you've forgotten something important. Also, having it written down reduces your subconscious mental harassment. It's a daily spring-cleaning of the mind really and takes only a few minutes to accomplish. Why not do it over a cup of coffee?

As I've said, it makes sense to tackle your list in the right order. Priority Number One is the return of the call to Alan Brown, your bread-and-butter client. You know you stand the best chance of catching him just after 9am, so don't leave until later, unless you have a good reason to do so. If you're an early riser you could number those negatives first and put them in-hand for printing. The bank isn't open until 9.30am, so go there after you've ordered the film. And why not get the envelopes (and the present) whilst you're at it? Check the car levels before you go. It's not yet 10am, and you now feel you are getting organised. A good feeling. Go to the lab next, remembering the new client has to be telephoned when you're in the right frame of mind, otherwise you could 'blow it'. Perhaps sometime in the afternoon, if you honestly think it's not desperate. Calls are cheaper after lunch anyhow.

By lunchtime things are different. Your first call to Alan Brown resulted in a request to go over after lunchtime for an hour of photography. Now your haircut will have to wait, but you might be free by late PM. By then a couple of new items are added to your list so, at the end of the day take stock of the situation once again, making a new list. 'Post-It' slips are ideal for this because they can be stuck onto any office wall, the dashboard of your car, or even the screen of your computer. Now you can feel you are getting somewhere!

A feeling of achievement, no matter how small, is a positive thing, and counts as a success. The day will go better and you will feel 'organised', another step has been made in the right direction.

Although not strictly a list, another good investment is to buy a pocket note-pad, not spiral-bound, which would encourage you to tear out pages, but staple-bound. Carry it with you, using it to scribble telephone orders, messages, and all the job information that you can't hope to memorise. Each entry you make must start with the date and client, with all relevant details about negative numbers etc. It is in this book that you record mileage travelled, materials used and time spent on jobs, plus anything else you think is important. I tried to manage without such a pad and ended up with scribbles on cigarette packets, on the back of receipts, even on parking tickets. At the end of a month there was much soul-searching and digging in waste-paper baskets in a futile attempt to bring together all the necessary information needed to build up an invoice. I know that hundreds of pounds can be lost through being inefficient in this way.

The more knowledgeable of you might say "Why not have a proper job-sheet, with all the necessary boxes to be filled in?" I agree, that's a great idea! But people are people, they are not perfect. Have your job-sheets printed by all means (I did) if you can afford it at the outset. But you will still need a note-pad because, chances are, when you sit in your car after completing a job, that job-sheet is back in the office.

After all my years as a photographer I feel I am reasonably well-organised now, as photographers go! But, in honesty and with hindsight, it wasn't until I acquired a computer that things really changed for the better. I originally justified its purchase because I had experienced a particularly good financial year and needed to spend some of my profits on something business-related to avoid paying too much tax. The computer was primarily intended to help with bookkeeping, invoicing and VAT so, naturally, I bought a program to do all that (computers are useless lumps of hardware without the software installed within them!). There's no doubt that becoming 'computerate' is much easier the younger you are but, after much burning of candles into the night, I eventually 'made friends' with it.

Before the computer, I thought I *was* organised but I soon realised I wasn't and the time spent learning how to use the thing was soon saved. Strangely, the spin-off advantages were not to be ignored either, even the salesman didn't tell me what it would do for me, as a person. My brain has always been active, but I had one of those grasshopper-minds that flits from subject to subject, whilst expecting everybody to keep up with my train of thought. In short, my mind wasn't disciplined. Those of you who understand something of the workings of a computer will realise that they are the ultimate organiser. Their memory is infallible and almost instant. They can also sort out lists of names or numbers at an astonishing rate and are ideal for your client and supplier telephone lists. My 'PC' had one of those so-called 'friendly' programs where I could see the information visually displayed in graphic filing-cabinet form. I could see at a glance how my files were stored and, in a way, it was like looking into its 'brain'. I soon related this to my own brain with its memory, ideas and information, and found that it was inadvertently teaching me to organise myself in a similar way. I now find there has been a great improvement in my overall organisational skill, though I'm still imperfect of course. Maybe we're only human but we do still have the ultimate edge over computers by being creative, sensitive and caring, and much more besides.

Time-planning and time-saving are often aided by some hi-tech gadget. Even on those days you have to travel long distances, the travelling time need not be wasted time. Planning can be done via a small portable tape-recorder and, if you have a mobile telephone, calls can be made and received 'on the move'. There is something extra-satisfying about taking a large order over the 'phone when you are away from the studio. There you are, perhaps fishing, or driving, or having a 'Little Chef' (or whatever) and the 'phone rings. That 'phone message could bring an order worth many hundreds of pounds, giving a feeling of doing something positive. Don't forget, you don't just have to be taking photographs to be productive. Some of my best work is done lying in the sun, apparently doing nothing but sun-bathing, but the brain is still working, planning, thinking and sometimes scheming.

Whether you are self-employed or not, whether you are operating as part of a team or completely solo, having time to assess your current situation and to plan ahead is a most important part of your business life; and it can be done anywhere. Most very successful businessmen confess their lives are controlled by work, and it has become the way of life they prefer. They still find time for leisure, but even then they keep a business-eye open for good opportunities. This 'affliction' sometimes causes the 'victim' to be called a work-aholic but, unless the side-effects are misery and miserliness (and you can still retain a decent sense of humour), there is no real harm done.

In your reflective moments if you are anticipating, for whatever reasons, a lull in business during the next few months, then plans ought to be made in advance to fill your future time effectively.

I have made all sorts of errors of judgment in my career, possibly the worst having been failure to look far enough ahead. When busy working seven days a week, we tend to think this state of affairs will continue forever, but this could be wishful thinking. Unless you have accumulated a large sum of money that will sustain you through hard times, you must always be mindful of the possibility that work could dry up, almost overnight. When you are worked off your feet it is difficult to imagine that eventuality, but it is precisely at these times you are likely to neglect your vital personal relationships with valued clients.

As part of my 'organising' I always have a list of my main clients close by me, but it also includes my old-but-less-regular customers, those who are 'growing-bigger' and potential big-spenders; and even a separate list of those particular companies I wish *were* my clients. It's not that I think I might forget who they are, and I don't write them down simply to remember them. There's an even more weird reason than that! Once or twice a week during my desk-bound moments (perhaps whilst I've stopped for a cup of coffee), I take out my list of names and companies and look at them one by one. Obviously, in reading the list, my mind conjures up mental images of the people mentioned, and I might wonder how old-so-and-so is getting on. Sometimes, less than five minutes later, that person will ring me on the telephone to ask if would mind doing a job for him! It doesn't happen every time, but I have lost count of the number of times it has!

Somehow, the act of visualisation transmits vibrations or thought waves that are received by the person in my thoughts. That's the only explanation I can give. Perhaps, when I visualise that person, and his mind isn't heavily involved with something else, he finds himself thinking of me and that he needs my services. It can be a little unnerving to have it happen often, but they do say that we all have powers we have forgotten how to use – this could be one of them. Try it yourself, being careful not to concentrate too hard, try to be quite relaxed about it. You have nothing to lose and plenty to gain! It works on personal friends as well!

We know, as businessmen, we are supposed to know every aspect of business procedure, including having plans for short-term policy and long-term projections concerning growth and cash flow, as covered by that relevant Chapter. In practise, most photographers do not look ahead, preferring to drive by the seat of their pants, maybe trusting to fate, luck, or faith in their ability and personal charm. After all, famous artists in days gone by surely didn't worry about business procedures! But these days, things have to be done differently, or we might end up penniless and starving in a garret (as *they* frequently did). Artistic or not, we cannot escape the need to be organised if we are to survive in our chosen profession. Better to accept that fact with some resignation and do our best to enjoy the feeling of 'being on top of things'. That way, we will be more relaxed about our actual photography and, as a result a better job. Indeed, we could probably even say we have that duty. We owe it to ourselves, our families and, where applicable, to our employees to be successful. Even in times of success comparative poverty can be lurking around the corner. To avoid this potential change in fortune please absorb my following 'never never' list;

1) never assume too much or take people for granted
2) never put all your eggs in one basket
3) never fail to promote new business
4) never neglect aged debtors for too long
5) never, never gossip, it comes back to you (have the diplomacy of a priest).
6) never knock the opposition
7) never stop trying to improve yourself

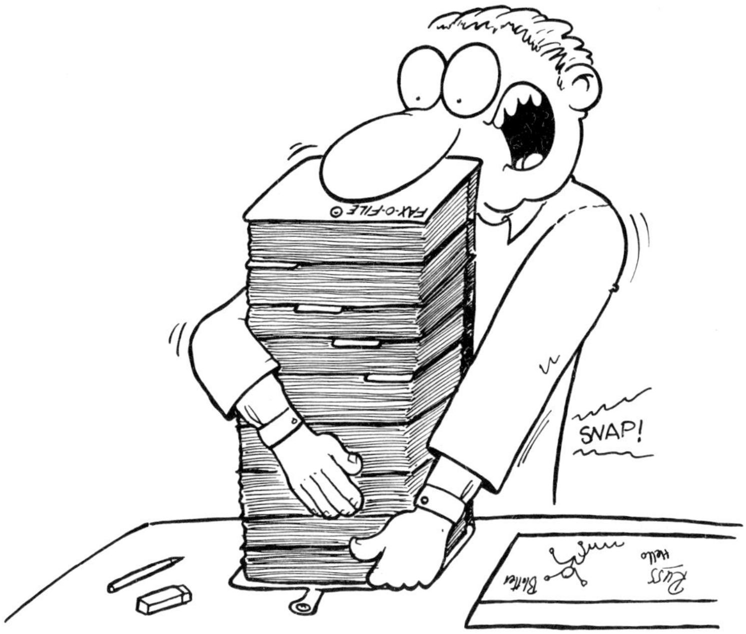

There are countless ways in which we can improve and organise ourselves and our business and I'm sure you will implement some of your own ideas once you have got the habit. Without this vital accessory you could end up like poor Vincent Van Gogh, creative and prolific, but miserable and quite mad. *With* the essential ingredient of 'organisation' you start to become a complete and self-assured operator, and no photographer can ever be called 'professional' without it!

CHAPTER SIX

Meeting People...and Caring.

Meeting People.

People *are* life! Without them, everything would be rather pointless and, as the song goes, "People, who need people, are the luckiest people in the World". You can still be a 'loner', but that pair-bonding drive will catch up with you in the end, but because of the nature of our profession we need people to exist at all!

One of the joys of being a photographer in general practice is the opportunities that arise to meet so many interesting people. For me this is one of the most compelling aspects of my work and I would go so far as to say that my own interest in pure photography would have waned after the first five years without this vital stimulus.

Looking back, I was a rather shy, introverted teenager, with no experience of the opposite sex, with no idea how to conduct myself in 'strange' company. In fact, the only thing I had 'going for me' was a proper respect for my elders (a rather out-dated attitude today, it seems). I guess I might have been regarded as a nice enough lad, willing to please, but without much drive or experience and certainly lacking charisma of any sort. With my country-boy upbringing, the only memorable part of my presence would have been a strong Norfolk accent. All this was to change quite quickly and painlessly, though I wasn't to know it at the time.

You see, it's almost impossible to be a photographer without being in the limelight to some extent. When you're setting up a tripod in town, disappearing under a focussing cloth like the man who starred in "The Fly" you are, in fact, putting on a free show for all those passers-by who have nothing else to do but watch the guy taking pictures, so you are bound to attract attention. Lorry drivers call inane comments out of their cabs, and you ignore them. There will be countless references to "Candid Camera", and the perennial "Watch the birdie!" or "Smile please!". Even, "Are you David Bailey?" (he's still a household name, bless him!). You name it, I've heard it! Now long-suffering, but I still manage a good-natured smile (but not at their originality). I smile philosophically to myself, at the predictability of some people. But it's harmless!

Yes, you are bound to attract people's attention, some will even stop to chat. Others, believe it or not, will mistake your tripod for a surveyor's theodolite and ask when you are going to start knocking down the buildings! Meeting people is certainly unlikely to be boring. I've even had people 'phone the police, thinking I was 'casing the joint' when I was photographing a bank. The only law I might have been breaking was that of causing an obstruction, something I diligently try not to do. Tripping up old ladies with my splayed tripod legs would not only be traumatic for the victims, but it could prove costly in financial compensation.

These days the focussing cloth and plate camera are a rarity on the streets but, if you have fears of 'performing in public', I can assure you these will quickly disappear. Photography is still a respectable profession, particularly with the likes of Lord Snowdon or Lord Lichfield earning their living at it, you are indeed in good company. More lately our Prince Andrew and other 'Royals' have added their contributions, endorsing the profession still further.

If your subject is a shop or a block of flats, for instance, there is always enough to do to keep your mind off any fears you might have of performing in public. You won't have time to wonder whether you look foolish, you will be too busy concentrating on composing your picture, filtering the clouds, or watching out for scruffy beaten-up old vans which have a habit of parking 'in frame' just as you've worked out your exposure.

When you are patiently waiting for the sun to re-appear, or for some rather interesting clouds to move into picture, you will sometimes welcome a little company, as light relief. And you have the type of job where almost anything can happen. The experiences I have had are too numerous (or lurid) to recount here, but I have been accosted a few times, have been kissed passionately by two beautiful ladies I had never met before (or since) and been flashed by both sexes more than once. I guess the camera brings out the exhibitionist in some people.

You see, as photographers, we are more than most, observers. Observers of life and human nature, its frailties and its humour. I quickly learned that life is too short to waste on what might have been, or could be. Shyness is merely a state of mind, an illusion.

For some people, walking a dog is an intro to conversation. The camera can have the same effect. It's certainly unlikely that with tripod and black-cloth you will be ignored. Each new day brings its challenges, with new people to meet and work with, and generally have fun and get paid for it! Sometimes you will only meet them once and, never having met them before (or ever likely to again) you can be just who you like, experimenting with conversation, ideas and techniques, both photographic and personality-wise.

When you are working on those techniques you will have good days, and some not so good but, eventually, your own style will develop, improving your 'bedside-manner', continually creating, discarding old ideas for newer, more successful ones. Not a day going by without ending up wiser. The unpredictability of each day, and what it throws at you, will soon become your way of life and most of your surprises will be nice ones. The speed at which things happen, and the diversity of subjects to look forward to, is almost unbelievable. A day can start looking unpromising, with the darkroom beckoning you to catch up with a few print orders, but by ten o'clock you could be fifty miles away, sunshine-roof open, a boot full of equipment and the Welsh hills in front of you.

And isn't the telephone a marvellous thing? How is it that Monday at 10am your diary is almost empty, but by 11am you are booked up for a week solid? Now your only worry is that, if the 'phone keeps ringing, how can you fit anything else in? But you will!

It was just such a Monday morning a few years ago when the 'phone rang, but no louder than usual.

Could I be at a factory location inside twenty minutes to photograph a VIP visitor? "Of course", was the reply from my end. Nothing unusual about the request, so I naturally asked who it was I had to photograph. "Can't say," he said, "just be there." So I was. Just a client with an over-dramatic approach to his normally hum-drum job, I thought, as I threw the flash-pack onto the rear seat of my car and drove in the direction of who-knows-what.

The client was there, as promised, looking worried and apprehensive and I wondered if perhaps I should as well. I didn't know how, so I didn't! But I wondered what, or who, had turned a normally placid man into this nervous wreck? He spoke, as if passing on secret information. Inside two minutes Edward Kennedy, brother of the Late President and himself campaign runner for the biggest job in the USA, would be there as part of an unannounced whistle-stop tour of the UK. Could I take plenty of pictures?

I did, of course. And when the 'big man' had gone half an hour later, my client had to sit down, the colour slowly returning to his cheeks but emotionally drained. He had something to tell his wife and kids – if he ever fully recovered he would relate his story many times, over a pint, the Christmas pudding, and to anybody he could make listen to his awesome tale on countless holidays in the years to come. He had the pictures to prove it. Another lesson learned about just a man, nothing more, and the 'ho-hah' that surrounds him.

The truth is, we have the sort of job where you can expect the unexpected to happen, so why act surprised or worried when it does?!

And there is absolutely no reason to be awe-struck. He wasn't a god, he is only flesh and blood, a human being, albeit world-famous. Acting nervously and running around like a headless chicken is expected of everybody else, but not us! We've seen it all before! It's part of our stock-in-trade to rub shoulders with Royalty and be on first name terms with the stars. We do our work to the best of our ability, regardless of who or what is involved. We know full well that losing our cool is counter productive and, whilst we always treat our subjects with respect and take our cue from them, we *are* the eyes of their public; the face they offer the camera is the one which we record for posterity, as our duty. We do not harass them, for we are not 'paparazzi' and we always respect their privacy.

I think our own gutter-press have done our image more harm than the squads of 'paparazzi' that plague the Continent, and beyond. At least we know who they are, but the fiends of Fleet Street, damaging rich and poor alike for the sake of a good story, seem oblivious to feelings and sensitivity, apparently making their own rules.

With Royalty there are stringent rules, made quite clear to us professionals at any Royal Occasion by the ever-present Press-Officer from the Palace. The police presence at such occasions can, and will, enforce such rules. It would be counter-productive to rock the boat, so conform and go along with all procedures and suggestions. Only a fool would jeopardise his future by getting black-listed! The watch-word is conformity, tempered with due respect.

It may sometimes seem unfair that you are not allowed to stand just where you would like to photograph a Royal but, at formal occasions, if everybody stood where they wanted the result would be a farce. The Press are given special dispensation by being allowed to stand at the front where they can see, even if they are corralled, at least they are all equal. If it was otherwise then the one who was rudest, and most selfish, would get the best pictures! If in doubt about the fairness of this, imagine what it would feel like if *you* were the Royal, or celebrity, in question.
Q.E.D.

In your new world of gaining professional experience you will accumulate quite a collection of new acquaintances. Many of the people who help you conduct your business are likely also to become your friends. They certainly should be treated as such, even though they may not become your drinking buddies. Whilst you are gathering your professional contacts around you, it is a good idea to systematically list them, in order that you might reach them at a minute's notice. I have a computer list of more than four-hundred contacts, built up over some years, and a print-out of these people with their telephone numbers, is always with me, even in my car or on location. But, if you're not yet computerate, a Filofax system works just as well.

My own list contains customers, suppliers, friends, (and my pet colour lab, of course) but, probably of equal importance though less-obvious, I include models or their agencies, hotels, helicopter-charter companies, restaurants, emergency services, insurance broker, motor-cycle couriers, Interflora, weather forecasting services, airlines, bank, accountant, and many more. I'm sure you could quickly make your own list! Mine gives me peace of mind, no matter where I am, and I feel that I am in touch at all times. Once a week I add new numbers to my ever-growing register and, because of the diversity of my contacts, I have been called "Mr Fix-it" more than once.

If you persevere with your professional attitude towards people then, within a short space of time, you could yourself become known as the photographer who 'keeps his cool', no matter how regal the company. These things have a habit of escalating, as you carve your niche in life. Without name-dropping, I modestly admit there are so many faces seen on television (and the 'big screen'), that have been before my camera, I wouldn't attempt to count them. Discretion forbids me to name them, but many are milestones in my own chequered life, representing memories that I value as much as my very profession. Yes, you can be 'cool' yet still be impressed! On the other hand, some are 'notorious', in some way or other, but they are still people.

In another chapter (Increased Sales..), I discuss "How we are Perceived", and I must admit that my own exploits with the famous have never done my own image any harm. On the contrary, there are those who awe-fully respect my own lifestyle more than is decent, but in turn, I'm only human!

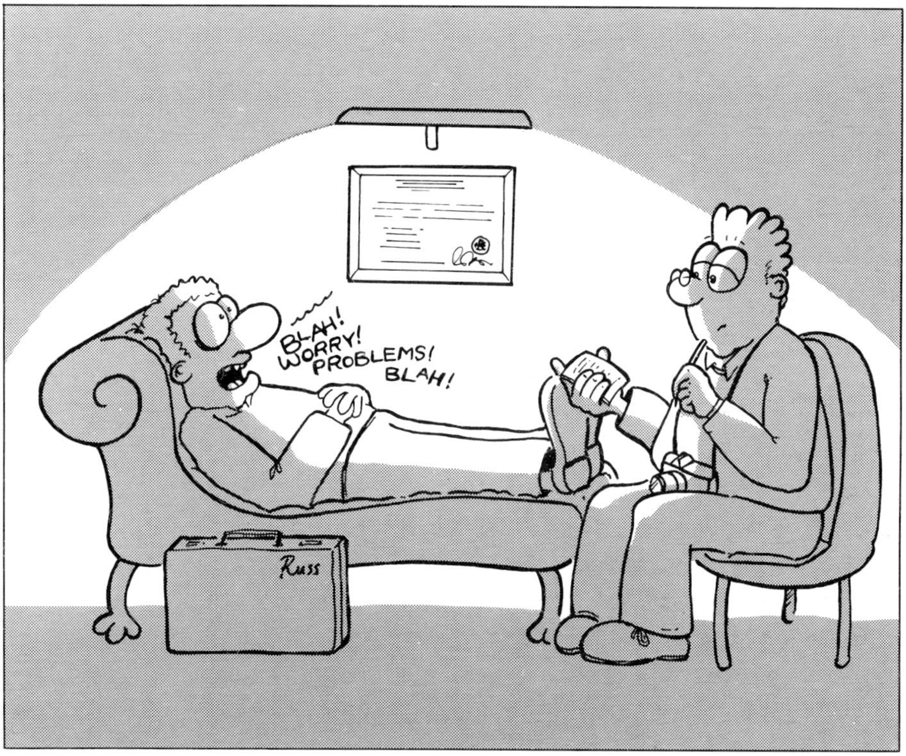

Caring!

Some years ago I noticed that a client was staying rather a long time on the 'phone, perhaps ten or fifteen minutes at a time. What he had to say relating to business could have been dealt with inside three minutes, but he really wanted a friendly chat as well. He was much older than me and had the reputation with some in our Company of being "a bit of an old woman". The truth was he was a nice guy who was going through some personal crisis and welcomed a friendly ear now and then. We didn't discuss the wife who didn't understand him, or how he feared getting old and losing his virility; it wasn't necessary. We spoke 'man talk', if there is such a thing, as you might in a pub. Eventually a senior member of our staff, who couldn't contain his annoyance any longer, asked why I let this bloke bend my ear. I froze the fellow with a look that would curdle milk. Actually, I didn't really know why I was human enough to "waste my time", I hadn't thought of it in that way, but it didn't cost anything to be civil and the client was paying for the call. However, it made me realise that my colleague had an entirely different attitude to mine, and he often made this transparently clear, both in words and in body language. He had a simple policy in life whereby he would only put himself out if there was something in it for him. Even his friends were 'used', until they wised up, or accepted him for what he was. In short, he was a 'taker'. But my patient attitude paid off for me, just as surely as if I had won the pools. Some eight years later, my old friend, now in a senior position with a large and successful national company, had put my name forward for a real peach of a job that was to become regular, and earn me tens of thousands of pounds each year, and it came at a time when I needed it most. Providence? More a case of "As you sow, so shall you reap!"

There are strange and powerful forces at work in this world of ours and I doubt if we shall ever understand them. I know my *ex*-colleague never will!

We are often expected to operate beyond the call of duty and I could relate dozens of instances when I have worked 'silly' hours for little return, hopeful that it would 'reserve a place for me in heaven'. I don't know about the after-life but these things have a habit of equalising themselves in the most amazing ways.

Putting yourself out can mean giving a client the benefit of your advice (something you're not being paid to do). For instance, perhaps he wants to buy a camera for his son's birthday and would like to know what's available for £100. He has a problem and is turning to friends for help, which is something we all do at times. Be as helpful as you can, being careful, of course, to leave the final decision of camera model to him. He won't pay for your advice but it should pay you in the long run, in reputation if nothing else!

Carrying the Can!

When a job doesn't turn out satisfactorily, not necessarily a write off, but not up to your usual standards, then you have something of a problem. If the results are not up to your expectations, will they be up to the client's? This hinges around the standards of excellence you have set yourself, how high they are, and how discerning the customer is. In truth, if your standards of acceptance are much lower than the client's, then he will go elsewhere for his next job. Perhaps he won't say anything to you, merely blaming his own bad judgment in choosing you for the assignment in the first place, and making a mental note not use you again.

It could be you excel at location work and are not too hot in the creative studio stakes. Does the client simply think you are not a lot of good generally? Without doubt we all have our strengths and weaknesses, tending to succeed in areas that come easiest to us. In other words, we are motivated by our own interests in a particular area.

As in all things, we are frightened of what we don't fully understand.

I used to hate certain studio jobs, like photographing machine tools, and I dreaded their arrival. They took three times as long as any other job and my first results weren't exactly my idea of perfection either. Creating shape, texture and interest in such subjects doesn't come easy, but with perseverance and considerable anguish I eventually 'cracked it' until, what was once a fear and a dread, became quite routine. Eventually I became expert in this particular field, and earned many thanks from a grateful client who, until my efforts, had traipsed around most of the photographic studios in the Midlands before contacting me.

In itself, this is a very satisfying experience, to know I had succeeded where others had failed, and a feeling of achievement, and even personal pride followed, making the struggle seem more worthwhile.

Naturally, resting on one's laurels is not the order of the day because there's always the next problem, and further goals to reach.

It is this constant striving for excellence that will separate you from the pack. Each mastered technique adds another feather to your cap, and your confidence grows daily. Confidence, but not complacency for, from my experience, the moment complacency creeps in, that is the dangerous period. Almost as though it invites disaster, like 'pride before a fall'. Not exactly superstition, but very close. For example, to boast that you are super-busy and making lots of money is inviting trouble, because some natural (or perhaps supernatural) law comes into force and can sweep it all away overnight. I don't know why it is, or why it happens that way. Perhaps the gods don't like us to be too cocky, so they promptly teach us a lesson of life.

Humility 'They' like, so play safe! Besides, if you've got your head down and are beavering away towards your next goal, you won't have time to 'pose'.

The Buck Stops with You!

When you are clawing your way up the professional ladder there will undoubtedly be times you will take chances. No matter how skilled you are, or may think you are, there will be days when you have your fingers crossed, knowing that you have pushed your luck just a little too far. Perhaps you have been under pressure from an overbearing client or art-director, and you have failed to be systematic or take all the usual steps to safeguard against failure, or the possibility of it. Not wanting to appear amateurish, you might have neglected to bracket your exposures when you should. You may even have loaded 64 ASA transparency film when the meter was set for 200 ASA, only noticing when reloading. What do you do? Do you confess your inadequacy and risk looking a fool? Do you make some excuse to retake the last frames again? Because if you have under-exposed by one and a half stops, you have got a wipe out. Or would you simply cross your fingers yet again and say nothing? My advise is, don't think crossing your fingers, or anything else, is going to make it right. You are going to look an even bigger fool if you get no results, not to mention the humiliation, or time wasted trying to put things right (even if it was possible).

What do you do? Of course, it rather depends on the prevailing mood of your client, and you would have to be super-smooth to get away with a full confession; though I might try it on a client who knows I don't make a habit of such things. So long as you are aware of the amount of over- or under-exposure, the lab *could* compensate in their processing. Throwing yourself at the mercy of a belligerent client can really only be done once or twice! Or, as a particular young artist/ layout lady frequently says, after witnessing a 'cock-up', "They can't actually kill you for it!" Which rather puts it in perspective, I suppose.

Two major lessons are to be learnt from all of this.

Firstly, to remove all doubt about your film-stock, and the processing of it, buy your film in bulk quantities of the same batch number from a reliable source. Then test-exposures can be made to check the recommended speed or any filtration needed. If your film supplier keeps his stocks in a hot warehouse, there is no point in you putting it straight into the 'fridge' when you get it. If you throw it on the back seat of your car and it fries in the sun you can't then blame those colour shifts on the lab. And always use a lab which prides itself on their quality control. One that processes control-strips daily, and carefully monitors all replenishment.

Secondly, and just as important for your peace of mind and professional status, approach each job as though it was a delicate operation totally dependent upon your expertise and know-how. Because it is. Plan whatever you can beforehand (do your homework). Don't be rushed, but work at the pace most comfortable for yourself. Some days that will be faster than others. Always keep calm and concentrate on the end goal.

Maintaining the Image.

If you must mix weddings and babies with commercial and industrial work keep *quiet* about it, or you are likely to drive away your big-spending commercial clients. This is a question of 'image', and big business must see you only as established and successful. The way you are 'perceived' by others is all-important. If a customer feels your skills are just right for him and that by engaging you, all his needs will be fulfilled, what else is there? As a manager he is only as good as the people he employs and having a caring and successful photographer at his disposal is a real feather in his cap. One less cause for concern!

When you are working for more than one client in the same field, absolute secrecy is vital to ensure your integrity is never brought into doubt. If you discuss a client's competitors with him, he will assume you are likely to do the same with others behind his back.

In fact, clients can even get possessive about *their* photographer, not wanting to share him (or her) with anyone, for fear of you not being available precisely when he needs you. Further evidence that each client likes to feel you are exclusively his. You can't be, of course, but the illusion is worth preserving and all that's needed is for you not to discuss your other work with him in detail, and always be available at the end of a telephone ready to attend to his every need without complaint. Naturally, you will be 'servicing' a dozen similar clients under the same circumstances.

In reality, he knows you do have other clients and, indeed, the reverence in which your services will be held depends, to some extent, upon your other successes in your field. It's something of a paradox where he expects you to be in great demand, but will always find time for him. Then his illusion is complete.

CHAPTER SEVEN

Pricing and Profits...£1000 a Day!

This is a subject which causes all photographers some considerable consternation, whether they are newly into professional photography or seasoned veterans. Their dilemma is that of fixing a pricing structure acceptable to clients whilst maintaining a healthy profit. Generalising, it is true to say that most established photographers *undercharge*, but keep their annual turnover figure looking respectable by virtue of the fact that they have a good core of regular clients, and the peaks and troughs average out. Known, by some, as a swings-and-roundabouts situation.

There is, of course, the danger that you will find yourself under-charging some very cost-conscious client, just to keep him 'sweet' and to get his work, and recoup those losses by over-charging another. That's not fair on you, and certainly not fair on the over-charged client. Please recognise that there will always be some 'horse-trader' trying to beat down your prices, sometimes as a matter of principle alone, and it's up to you whether you fall into this trap – because it will happen. Unfortunately, it is those same people who haggle when you present your invoice. Learn to recognise the rather obvious signs and be on your guard, but don't be tempted to drop your prices too much, too often. This is one area where it might be necessary for you to get bitten before you learn the lesson, because these people come in many guises. Just make sure you don't lose too much. If all of your customers were allowed special rock-bottom prices, with little or no profit margins, then you would find yourself rushing around trying to make sufficient money just to pay your on-going overheads. This is known as the 'busy-fool' syndrome, I'm sure you can see why!

Fortunately, the majority of clients are quite familiar with photographers' professional charges and 'play the game' but, if they are not conversant with the 'going rate', it is up to the photographer to gently educate them. Politely, of course!

In a way, the newly-established, up-and-coming photographer has an advantage over the veteran for, when a new business is born the pricing structure is created with it. Whilst our long-standing businessman fixed his pricing system many years ago and, apart from adding a few percent every year or so, dare not rock the boat by seriously increasing his prices for fear of causing the migration of his clientele. Again, it's an attitude problem. *There's a psychology in pricing that can't be ignored.* The photographer doesn't want to lose what he has already got, so he plays safe. He would rather 'survive' than take the risk of losing his regular bread-and-butter clients.

Also, he vividly remembers some very lean periods in his business history. Maybe a recession or two; a depressed economy, or a period of national strikes and short-working weeks. He possibly survived those traumatic times by eating away at any financial buffer he might have built up; or perhaps by taking out a loan, in the hope of better times ahead. Maybe he sold his car and drove a more frugal one. But, he survived .....and only just, by relying on providence and the see-sawing of national business fortunes. Sensible pricing structures could have avoided this.

Please don't think I'm knocking our established professionals, how can I when I'm talking from my own painful experience. I was there in the bad old days, along with my contemporaries; doing it all wrong. But wisdom in hindsight is better than none at all. The worst part was the valuable time wasted. When I 'got it wrong', it sometimes took several traumatic years to rectify the situation. Naturally it cost money too, but time cannot be replaced. They say that we all have to make our own mistakes, but one of the purposes of this book is to try and prevent people making the same old *classic* ones. Life is indeed too short for that luxury. Whilst we cannot guarantee we will avoid mistakes completely, we should do everything in our power to analyse our own potential weaknesses and, because this chapter is dedicated to pricing, we must be talking about money, and our own attitude towards it. I'll say it again. Money!

There are those amongst us who have a *problem* with that word and I can understand that but, being practical, we must realise that we can't survive in business without it, no matter how charitable we might like to be. Can we get that particular ghost laid, right here and now? By doing so perhaps by the end of this chapter you will have a better understanding of one of the most important aspects of professional photography, that of putting money in its proper perspective so that you can concentrate on taking pictures.

Do you have a problem when looking another person in the eye when talking money? Do you avoid the subject or get embarrassed when it crops up? Many people do and that is why the majority of financial negotiations take place over the telephone. If a price has to be agreed, far better to get it out of the way before you start and, if you can't do this easily 'off the top of your head', you must work out your strategy on paper beforehand.

Here we are talking about our daily rate (the price that we consider our services to be worth) and an hourly rate, materials and processing, reprint prices, travelling costs, and other expenses, not forgetting our percentage mark-up on anything we buy-in or shop-out. Herein lies the success, or otherwise, of our business. No matter how fine a photographer you are, unless your pricing structure is right for the part of the country in which you operate, you could be making your life much more difficult than it need be, missing out on an awful lot. Certainly it will decide your image, and your lifestyle, or whether you are destined to waste valuable time and nervous energy sorting out one financial crisis after another. And that's the last thing you want!

A good profit-margin decides the equipment you use, the car you drive, the holidays you take, and the clothes you wear. In fact it controls almost everything in your business and private lives that you can think of; including your peace of mind and ultimately, even your health to some extent. Being too coy about making a profit will undoubtedly cause you to 'repent at leisure'. Without decent profit margins, you will not only suffer in all the above-mentioned ways, but you will be jeopardising your very existence, and your demise from the photographic scene will deprive all your clients of your services, possibly forever. So come to terms with it and decide *Rich is Best*. Remember, poor people worry and go without, or get into even more debt in their desperation to survive.

Now let us go back to the beginning, and set up our pricing structure, remembering that if you already have one, it's not too late to change it.

Start by finding out what others charge. This can be done by ringing round, or by getting somebody else to do it for you. Create a fictitious job to obtain a quote, preferably over the telephone. You'll soon get a good picture of the current situation and you will be struck by the difference between the lowest and the highest fees charged!

Day-rates might vary from as low as £50 per day, up to £1000 per day. Ignore the low quotes – they're a joke! No self-respecting photographer can work for these silly figures, unless he is already 'on the dole', moon-lighting, or totally desperate. Put yourself in the position of a genuine client who is conducting the same exercise. Low quotes are ignored, always being treated with suspicion. At the very best, he will conclude that the photographer has such a low opinion of himself, his worth is reflected in his fees. The sky-high quotes are invariably from city-based operators who either have to cover their high city-overheads, or perhaps have an inflated opinion of themselves. Some are rip-off merchants cashing-in on the 'city image', but others genuinely operate in certain specialised fields where such high figures are common-place. Perhaps they are even worth it, on a value-for-money scale. City-based or otherwise, very high day-rates are always accompanied by equally high peripheral charges (for prints and other ancillary services) but the price is right so long as there are people willing to pay it. Let me give you an example which I think demonstrates one of the most important lessons to be learned in the world of business today.

When compact discs first came onto the hi-fi music market, they were very expensive and this was justified by the superlative quality of musical reproduction when compared to cassette tapes and vinyl records. Recording companies also claimed that they had to recover the millions it took to develop the new system (even though the research and development was done by only one or two major companies). After a year or so, it was expected that the prices would tumble as production and sales increased. Despite complaints from the general public, and from the music journals on their behalf, the prices didn't fall, even though the total production costs were probably less than £2.00 for an item selling for ten to twelve pounds. When interviewed, a spokesman for a major recording company shocked everybody by saying that the prices would not fall. His company invariably fixed their prices by supply and demand and, so long as there were people willing to buy their product at the present price, it indicated to them that *the price was right*. In a true marketing sense it was. The appearance of digital tapes might force a change of heart eventually but, in the meantime, manufacturers, middle-men and retailers all do very nicely, thank you.

So photographers, likewise, who have the world beating a path to their door will, naturally, charge as much as they think they can get away with, but have to be mindful of the 'value-for-money' argument. On the odd occasion that I have had to explain my prices to a curious client, I always maintain that they, as a Company, are also getting value-for-money on the following points.

Firstly, they are assured of results that achieve the desired effect in the shortest possible time, thereby keeping costs to a minimum. As caring, thinking photographers we should be aware that, when a client commissions us to help in his promotion, whatever it might be, our end product must 'work' for him. Secondly, our photographic efforts will increase his sales to a point where they easily recover our own professional fees. Thirdly, if we have achieved all of our objectives, we will also be enhancing that Company's standing and image 'in the market-place' whilst simultaneously raising the morale of its work-force. (A new brochure really can engender those patriotic feelings).

All this is true, no more so than when our photography is part of a Company's exhibition or brochure which has been properly designed with these criteria in mind. This, in my opinion, is value for money and, when saying so, I believe it and so does my client. He can't really argue about an investment of a few hundred pounds when it will generate several thousands in new sales and also improve his Company's image in the long-term. If we follow this policy, we should never need to feel guilty about our pricing, however high. However, in practice, though, we do on occasion have to compromise a little, showing our client we can be flexible. We should always be able to find reasons why we can do one job at one price and follow it up with a 'special offer' if there are special circumstances, always being careful not to create too much of a precedent.

Once a certain degree of trust has been established between you and the client, there can be years between discussions on fees, so long as you continue to satisfy him in that special value-for-money way.

By way of parable, I have one particular client who is well known for his 'carefulness', where as money is concerned. He manages to complain every time I see him about the price of everything, including my fees from time to time. Over the twenty-year period he has been my client, that's a lot of moaning! (This guy even moans because I *occasionally* stop to reload the camera with film.) Recently, as a result of some price reviews I had been doing, I decided it was his turn for a substantial 'rise', but felt apprehensive about his reaction.

I weighed the pros and cons. Why has he kept me on as his photographer for twenty-plus years if he's not satisfied?

He obviously was! If he wasn't happy with my results, he would have made other arrangements years ago (he's that sort). He even expects me to plan my holidays around his work, booking 'slots' months ahead. Could *this* be a guy who has real difficulty in giving compliments because it might cause price increases? The truth emerged! There was nobody else that would put up with this fellow for a day, never mind twenty years! Also, there was no other photographer who knew this client's subject better than I did. In short, he was stuck with me, as I was with him! I tolerated him because he paid quickly, despite his moaning and because, underneath his incessant complaining, was a human being who had somehow grown on me. Then I learned that, thanks to my pictures costing him about five-hundred pounds a day, he always stood to make at least ten-thousand. This really was worth a sizable price increase in my day-rate! Next time he telephoned to book a two-day job I broke the news to him. He paused for a second, and said OK! As cheerfully as he could, at least! This psychology thing really does work!

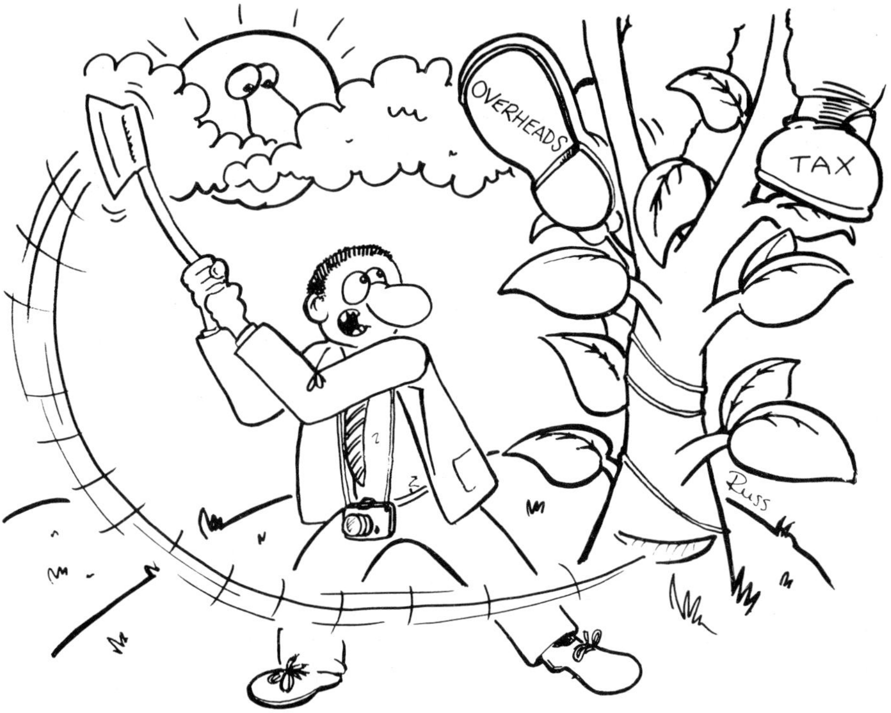

'ALL BECAUSE I DIDN'T KNOW BEANS FROM MONEY!'

£1000 a Day?

We can see, from the previous section on "Pricing" that, with no stretch of the imagination, we can easily make a thousand pounds each week, so long as we have the continuity of work. Let's face it, merely working for three days during one week, and including peripheral profits on film, prints and other expenses, we can readily improve that figure.

But did you know it is entirely possible to make £1000, or more, *in one day*?

I can assure you that this is done with astonishing regularity. Not every day, of course but, as you might appreciate, this is not necessary! I will give you a typical example of how it can be achieved!

Long Summer days have daylight hours from about 4am until 9.30pm, or thereabouts, and are ideal for architectural, or other exteriors. If you get up early and leave base at 5.30am, your time *then* starts clocking-up. By 7.30am you have travelled more than a hundred miles, having had a nice, pleasant journey avoiding rush hour traffic. You are 'on-site' and shooting exteriors as soon as the light is right. Take time off for breakfast if you like, then do some more photography before setting off on the second leg of your itinerary, a site some 90 miles away in a different direction. Weather still good, you continue your operating programme until lunchtime (or maybe work through if the conditions demand it), getting lots of creative pictures in the bag. Next stop 110 miles away, to complete another side of a geographical rectangle. Repeat performance, with light still on your side until sunset, when you take advantage of this God-given photo-opportunity, using the sunset as a backdrop. Photography finished, you head for home, grabbing a well-deserved late lunch/tea/supper on the way.

Whilst waiting for your meal to arrive, you jot down all relevant details of your long day, including time spent, materials consumed, miles travelled, etc.

You charge £350 per day, but this working 'day' has been 14 hours long. So, £350 divided by eight (hours), multiplied by fourteen, equals £612.50. You have, in fact, done the equivalent of two days work as far as the client is concerned, and it would have taken most people two whole days to complete what you have done but, by getting up early and taking advantage of the good weather (that you knew was in the offing), you have achieved your objectives in record time and saved your client the extra travelling costs of a second day. You may have been lucky with the weather, but you were *there* to take advantage of it. The rest was up to you; you put yourself out, you should reap the just rewards.

So far, we have accounted for earnings on all your time of £612.50. You are also charging for mileage, as per the AA/RAC guidelines, 350 miles at 28p per mile (minimum charge), allowing almost £28 costs for petrol consumed, giving a 'profit' of £70. You also mark-up your materials and print costs, 150 colour prints with a profit of only two pounds per print, makes a further £300. Total so far £982, and there are other areas of hidden earnings to include. Like the inevitable reprints the client will order in a few days time; or maybe some other expense we haven't mentioned, marked-up, of course. As a bonus, whilst you were out, your mobile 'phone rang – with a big order for prints from a previous job. The profit on them was a few hundred pounds, that had come right out of the blue, totally unpredicted, but nice.

You may be too tired to get excited about it (add it up yourself) as you have to get up early the next day again, going off in an entirely different direction, and so it goes on. I call it 'making hay while the sun shines'.

Those halcyon summer days make up for the dismally-short winter ones when you should be utilising the studio more. So, with a little bit of good fortune, and the weather-gods on your side, your £1000 per week could easily be three times that amount. Working weekends, as we must if the conditions dictate, will be a further bonus. If the work is there (and a certain chapter of this book ensures that it is) you can see that a weekly turnover of five or six thousand pounds is quite possible; if you have the energy!

Even in the studio, you can make similar amounts in Winter, if you are thus motivated and keep an eye open for the opportunity.

When you have organised your studio in such a way that photography is made as controllable, and as efficient as possible, it's amazing what you can achieve in just one day.

Before the days of 'hazylights', that soft directional light-source effect was produced by reflectors, tissue-paper, or an umbrella-type bounced light set-up that resembled a shanty-town construction in your studio. I'm not saying the results weren't excellent, but the path to success was laborious, to say the least. I know there are photographers who say, "That sort of training is good for experience." but, when purpose-built hazylights came onto the market, the whole complexion of things changed. It was then possible to do pack-shots in a fraction of the time previously spent. If the client was present, it became necessary to make the process look more difficult than it really was. Far better to be left to your own devices, so that the customer did not witness the speed in which it was possible to work. You could still add your catch-lights, or improvise in any way you wished, but hazylights made your job quite embarrassingly easy.

Because you are good at your job, or because you have some precious piece of equipment to make life easier, that is your good fortune, and your good judgment in buying wisely. Any equipment investment you make *should* create more efficiency, and produce better sales growth. If a client briefs you on a job, and you estimate that it could take less than a day to achieve the desired results, do you say so? If your client believes you have upwards of two days work ahead of you, why argue with him? He might be right. If he's not, then it's to your benefit.

Suppose you are in the business of putting out oil-well fires and you are asked to quote to extinguish a particularly tricky one. Your quote is accepted and, thanks to your ingenuity and expertise, you succeed in a couple of hours when it was expected to take a week. Because you 'delivered the goods' how can the client complain? Producing the right results, on time, is the essence of some work.

Another area of potentially high profits is aerial photography and, although some might consider it a specialised field, it's really not that difficult (as explained fully in the chapter on that particular subject). The beauty of it is, because it seems so hazardous and specialised, it commands a higher hourly and daily rate, and there are tremendous opportunities for respectable profit margins. For a start, you can increase your usual operating rates by anything up to fifty percent, depending on the client and what he's used to paying, so maybe five-hundred pounds per day would be a good starting point. That's all profit, of course, although it takes into account your usual on-going overheads. That is your time only, the helicopter hire in extra. Incidentally, some photographers calculate their hourly rate by dividing their normal eight-hour daily rate by seven (rather than eight) to allow for the nuisance of chopping their day about.

Next area of profit is the helicopter itself which, for this example, we will say is normally four-hundred pounds per hour, and which you have cleverly negotiated for three-hundred and twenty pounds per hour. Because, as an aerial photographer, you are potentially a very good customer for the helicopter charter companies, and good regular customers get special rates. You don't necessarily have to pass on those negotiated lower rates to your client.

You will realise that you are now making more profit from the helicopter hire than for your own operating time. You are making over one-hundred-and-fifty pounds per hour for every hour you fly. Allowing for the fact that you seldom need to fly more than six hours in any one day, but you would expect to be involved in non-flying planning and liaison for a couple of hours, you stand to make five-hundred on your day-rate plus four-hundred-and-eighty from your mark-up on the helicopter. On top of that you could easily be making another two-hundred pounds on prints, and a similar amount on other expenses. So far you are having a good day. If you were *really* greedy you could charge your client for hiring a 'Jet Ranger' helicopter at four-hundred pound per hour, but actually fly in the smaller (and cheaper) 'Robinson' at half the cost. You would then be making over two-hundred-and-seventy pound *per hour* (plus prints, etc). I wouldn't do it, and it sounds almost fraudulent, but some might try it!

I should like to point out that, even though the foregoing revelations are factual, even I am reluctant to disclose this startling truth, and I ask myself "Why?". The answer is, of course, "For the same reason as you ought to keep such things to *yourself*!". Earning such high day-rates, and admitting to such handsome profits, is not something you really want to shout about, but keep rather secret. Not from a tax point of view, you understand, but you should *never* give your clients the impression that you are 'coining it'. Nor even your friends! Humility is a far better image to cultivate than filthy-rich. Even so, I truly hope that my own clients don't read this. Perhaps *you* should only read it in bed!

Some elitist portrait photographers take great pride in achieving what they call "£1000 sittings". This means the revenue from one 'sitting' fee and, presumably, the subsequent prints, frames etc., total that 'magic' figure. To celebrate this achievement they have formed a club for all to enviously look upon. What they do at this club I don't know; I can only surmise it's a place they can boast to each other about how well they are doing. Personally, I don't see the point!

From my experience, pride definitely comes before a fall and, superstition or not, I'd rather not take the chance.

I prefer to keep a low profile in most things, though the writing of this book has to be an exception, because my mother told me, "It's alright to be better than others, if you can, but never tell them so!"

CHAPTER EIGHT

Invoicing, Credit Control and Finance

Stationery.

There is no way you can operate satisfactorily, or with credibility, unless you prepare proper invoices for services rendered. Naturally, a properly printed A4 sheet of stationery is desirable, though there is no reason why you cannot use just one item of stationery for all office work. The same style of 'headed' notepaper can function just as well for invoices as it does for letter-writing, or even quotations. This sheet of stationery has to show your business name and full address, telephone number and, if you have one, your fax number. You *can* live without a fax machine, unless your clients are totally fax-orientated and, personally, I would sooner spend my money on a cellular telephone. Neither is cheap to run unless you make it a policy to receive, rather than make, the connection.

If you intend to be VAT registered (when turning-over more than £35,000 per annum you **must**) you will need your VAT number printed somewhere on your invoice, but this can be quite small at the bottom of the page. Then, if you don't like it appearing on any non-invoice application, trim it off.

Some people manage to put all the necessary information at the top (or the bottom), of the A4 letterhead, then it is possible to have narrow "With Compliments" slips etc printed off the same artwork. Those franchised High Street printers will do this for you, and you can have as few, or as many, as you like, though larger quantities come cheaper.

Invoice Layout.

Invoice layout may seem pretty straightforward to some but let's have a look at it anyway, because there are good reasons for re-thinking this apparently simple task. Bear with me.

Somewhere top left goes the name and address of your client.

New Town Gears Ltd	
Hill House Works	8th May 1992
Garage Street	Our ref: 001
Micklesborough	Your ref: John Wells
Yorkshire SJ9 10XS	Purchase Ord.No.77777

On a similar level at the top right appears three important pieces of information. The date of invoice (Tax Point), your own reference number, and your client's reference. One above the other in the order mentioned, all neatly lined up, of course. Your own reference number is simply the number you have given that particular invoice. Each invoice has to have its own number for bookkeeping and other accountancy purposes so start as you mean to go on or you will regret it later, particularly if you are trying to track down an invoice or, worse still, have to ring up the accounts department of one of your clients and can't quote an invoice number. Firstly, you will be embarrassed at your own lack of system because everybody numbers invoices and, secondly, you will be upset when you have to wait longer for your money because you tried to 'buck the system'. Start your numbering system at 001, for example and, after a few years when you get to number 999, you can either continue on to 9999 or restart at 001. By that time you will have found the value of invoice numbers and maybe will have implemented a few other ideas of your own too, making your system work smoothly.

The 'customer reference' is merely to assist the recipient accounts department in finding an originator for your invoice. Somebody who works for the Company was instrumental in hiring your services which resulted in your invoice or, better still, he sent you an Official Order with its own number and this is where you quote that number so that your invoice can be matched to *their* copy of the Official Order (or Purchase Order). Doing this speeds up payment or, in some cases, means you get paid at all!

Larger companies just won't pay unless you have that magical "Official Order Number", so don't risk sending invoices without a relevant customer reference. You may even have a 'blanket order' number when work is contracted to you over a long steady period. This is nice, because your customer's accounts department gets used to seeing your invoices with the familiar number, and know the invoice to be bona fide. Thus, payment is made promptly and regularly. Even if they keep you waiting a couple of months you will have an on-going situation with money coming in at a regular date each month after an initial wait. It's a little bit like working a week in-hand; you get it in the end.

So far, we've only discussed the heading that accompanies all invoices. Now to the main body of the document and its relevant costing. Where applicable, you must start your invoice with a brief title that supplements the customer reference. When the originator of your work sees your invoice, as he undoubtedly will, to signature his agreement to his accounts department that the work was in fact carried out, he needs to be prompted as to what the invoice was for. If you took pictures of a new truck or machine on May 8th 1992, tell him so. "Colour and B&W photographs of new lathe taken on May 8th, 1992, as directed by Mr...". You are simply reminding him what it was he asked you to do, reminding him of his instructions reinforces his involvement in the final invoice. He deserves the credit, or the blame, for his part in it. Following the title go straight into costing:

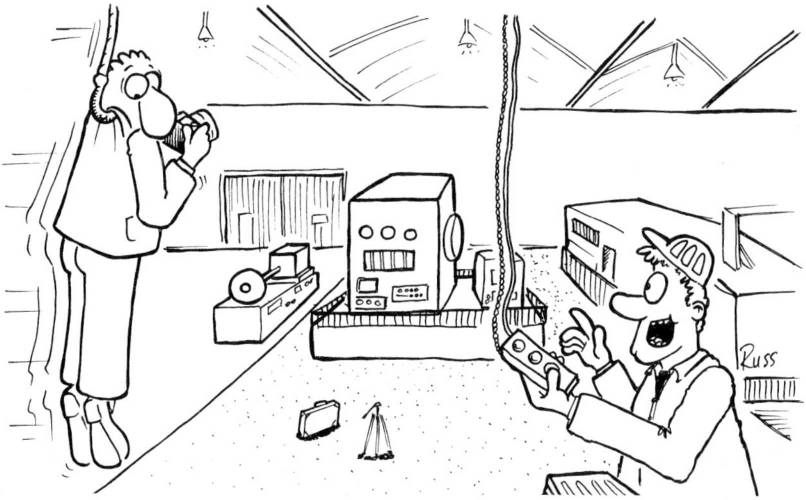

"Colour and B&W photography of new lathe taken on: 8th May 1992, as directed by Mr John Wells.

Three hours operating at £40.00 per hour .... £ 120.00

Materials & processing:
Three rolls 120 B&W film at £9.50 per roll .... £ 28.50
Two rolls 120 transp. film at £10.50 per roll .... £ 21.00
25 colour prints 10″ × 8″ at £4.00 each .... £ 100.00
B&W contact prints: 3 sheets at £6.00 ea .... £ 18.00

Expenses and travelling costs:
225 miles at 30p per mile .... £ 67.50
Background paper at cost .... £ 11.50

£ 366.50
VAT @ 17.5 percent £ 64.14

£ 430.64

Terms Strictly 28 Day Please.

(You will, of course, need a duplicate of this for your own files, so don't forget the carbon paper if it's being typed).

Having added-up all charges you may feel it appears slightly expensive for what you did, or perhaps think the client might find it a little 'out of proportion'. If so, then put in a 'sweetener' as a footnote.

eg; "No charge for liaison, or delivery on this occasion"

Possibly some more knowledgeable readers might say, "If you charge for film then you lose ownership rights of the negatives!"

Your decision here has to be balanced by each customer's specific needs. For instance, in supplying transparencies you have no 'original' on your files and, therefore, usually lose reprint sales. Often with black and white photographs of a non-creative nature there will be no re-print value in the negatives anyway. My policy is to charge the customer all time, materials and processing, rather than 'hide' the film cost within the hourly rate, then the customer can at least see what's going on!

If a job takes two-and-a-half hours, don't charge for three, at least not if the client was with you! Never be made to look dishonest, always monitor operating times carefully, you may have to justify your charges later. If you are honest, you soon get a good reputation and clients will accept your word as gospel. If you are caught trying to fiddle an extra hour here and there, make no mistake, your invoices will be scrutinised every time, assuming the customer stays with you.

Because this book contains a special section devoted to pricing, we will leave "invoicing" here and look at other office duties.

Credit where Credit is Due!

When you are in the big-money league, you can forget the old wedding days when cash was the name of the game. Nothing beats cash of course. It's real, it's tangible, it's safe and it is, from what I have sometimes heard, tax-free. However, I am not here to pontificate the whys and wherefores of tax evasion, that's between you and your conscience (and the tax man of course). Suffice to say if you get away with it in the short term, have no doubt your 'sins' will eventually find you out! The arm of the tax-man is longer than the arm of the law; and the law, incidentally, is very much on their side.

Big-money commercial clients do not deal in cash. They don't understand 'readies', seldom entertaining real money excepting on a petty-cash basis. Even then it all has to be accounted for down to the last penny. Please accept that you are firmly in the world of cash flow, creditors and debtors, and have to fit in with your customer's own individual payment terms.

Credit is expected, according to the company's own policy of payment and, be it monthly or three-monthly (or longer), you have to wait until your turn comes around, unless you have negotiated some special arrangement. In a few cases, payment is 'by return' but this is the exception rather than the rule, meaning you will be paid as soon as they receive your invoice, enter it in their bookkeeping system, raise a cheque in the accounts department and get it signed by one, or maybe two, signatories. Then it is posted off to you after only waiting a week if you are extremely lucky, and that is the best you can expect, and as near to cash on the nail as you will experience. Such efficient and thoroughly liquid companies are the exception. The others, the large proportion of debtors, will take a good deal longer, often ignoring the bit at the bottom of your invoice that says "Payment within twenty-eight days, please".

Business-men take deferred payment as a matter of course. If you want to improve on a client's usual procedure you will have to take up with their accounts department. It might help if you are on very good terms with the boss, or even the person who raises cheques. You might even see to it that the terms of your business are clearly stated on the reverse side of every invoice. In accepting your invoice, they would automatically be accepting your terms, unless they have written to you making other arrangements. This can take the form of a letter asking you to accept a compromise or comply with their company policy. But, whatever happens, you will always be owed money.

After a while, you will come to know which clients take their time and which ones play the game fairly. Philosophically, you can't really blame some debtors for taking as much time as they can get away with. After all, until their money is sitting in your bank account, it has not gone from theirs. They *could* hang on for six months, if you let them. You must not ignore this situation thinking it will all come right in the end! It may not! Also, allowing the situation to continue, either because you are not desperate for money or because you are too busy doing other things, is not a the answer either.

If your 'grapevine' is slow-working, you could find that one of your major debtors, a hitherto valued client of impeccable pedigree, has suddenly fallen on hard times and you may have joined a long list of their 'unsecured' creditors who will never get a penny owed to them. Unfortunately, every businessman eventually learns this lesson the hard way. The first you will know about it is a letter in the morning post from the appointed liquidator.

It will be short, to the point – and painful. It will simply tell you that you are on the list of creditors of the fallen company and, some day in the distant future, there will be a creditors' meeting. At this meeting you will inevitably be told that, after the secured creditors have been paid (usually banks, the tax-man and the liquidators themselves) there will be nothing left for you. Occasionally, you will be paid a few pence in the pound at most.

Statements.

At a predetermined time after invoicing, usually one month or at the end of a month, a statement can be sent out. This statement lists all outstanding invoices without going into detail, showing costs for each transaction with their respective invoice numbers. The statement can also show date and amount of the last payment received from the client, with the 'bottom line' showing the total amount outstanding (the balance).

Some people put the amounts in special 'boxes' in the stationery layout, indicating the amount for the current month, one month old, two months old and so on. The danger is this broken-down record can encourage people to only pay the most overdue invoices, yet another delaying tactic to pay as little as possible, as late as possible.

If you adopt the routine of sending out statements, not a huge chore if you employ a computer, then it could be that your client comes to expect your statement and will only pay after the receipt of same. For many years, since working 'solo', I have managed without sending out statements and, similarly, my customers have adjusted to not receiving any from me. For those slow-paying customers I make a 'phone call to the right person. For each customer I have a credit-rating stored in my head. This credit rating is based upon their own track record and my personal judgment, and can be affected by rumour (the grapevine), the amount in question and, to some extent, a gut-feeling.

A Likely Story!

Strangely, I have far more trouble trying to extract payment from clients who are members of the general public than I ever do from businesses. Unfortunately, you can't always judge people on face-value so, when accepting work from a new customer, you either have to ask for trade references or even do a 'search' on them. There are quite a few companies offering a search service and if large sums of money are likely to be involved, it could be wise.

Although these services exist, we are still, occasionally, caught out because we give people the benefit of the doubt.

Experience may teach us that taking on client's credit-worthiness for granted can be a costly mistake.

Suspicion can often be raised when attempting to 'chase' money by telephone. You decide to 'chase' a particularly overdue account and, when you give the invoice number, they say they have no evidence of your invoice, could you please send a duplicate. They may even say a cheque has already been sent and ask you to wait a couple of days to see if this fictitious cheque arrives. Of course, it won't! A few days later you ring back and they mumble about the inefficiency of the Post Office, saying they will stop the cheque in case it has been stolen and, if it arrives in the meantime, you should return it to them. Meanwhile (they say) they will raise another cheque and, having obtained the necessary signatures, post it off immediately.

A week later, you ring again only to be told one of the directors is on holiday and he didn't sign enough cheques before he left, so you will have to wait another two weeks until he returns. A month of procrastination has gone by, you are trying to be patient, they sound apologetic and as helpful as can be!

Two weeks later you ring yet again. There is no reply because the 'phone is dead. You try again later, thinking it could be a line fault and, this time, somebody answers. It's the liquidator; sounding like an undertaker! He's sitting in the same office you spoke to earlier, winding up affairs. As a creditor, you are told you will soon receive a letter about the creditors meeting....

You sit back in your swivel chair and the truth dawns. They *knew* all along the Company was in dire straits, they were just playing for time. The same story, or versions of it, has been told to hundreds, and you fell for it! Those sweet girls sounded so *plausible*!

Some people will send you a cheque but purposely will make sure the figures don't agree with the written sum, just to delay payment. Accounts staff, in large companies like the Gas Boards, pass their spare time compiling lists of excuses given for non-payment that read like a comedy sketch. But none of this is funny when you get caught yourself! Luckily, it doesn't happen too often if you take the proper precautions.

Credit Control.

Most photographers would like to live a life without the fuss of invoicing and paperwork. They usually consider it a tedious chore and, compared to photography, it is. If we are lucky, or completely organised, we would have a nice, kind person coming in regularly to sort out this side of things for us, letting us get on with what we do best. Unfortunately credit control has to be done so, unless we marry an accountant-type person, we are probably stuck with it. In which case we should try to make it as simple as possible.

An assignment is successfully accomplished, the relevant information pulled together and an invoice produced clearly stating the client's financial indebtedness. Almost always the cheque will eventually find its way to your letter-box without a hitch. You have a simple system of bookkeeping that 'logs' each stage of this 'anatomy of a cheque', including the triumphant lodging of the money into the relevant bank account. But what of those 'delinquent' few percent that seem so slow to pay?

Because we can quickly produce a summary of outstanding debtors from our 'books' (or, if we are computerised, at the touch of a few buttons), we always know the total amount we are owed, and how 'old' those amounts are. We list them in monthly order so we can see at a glance which ones are overdue, and by how long.

From my experience a simple telephone call to the right person can rectify the situation. It might be to a member of your client's admin staff (whom you know by name), a key member of the management or maybe the boss himself.

Don't feel guilty about asking for money owed to you. This is an accepted part of all businesses and shouldn't create any animosity at all. You simply need to know when you can expect a cheque and you could remind them that small, emergent businesses frequently have cash-flow problems, and need reasonably quick payment to survive. Never come across as being rude (or totally desperate) but be precise and pleasant about it. One 'phone call lasting about a minute should do the trick. Note the date you 'chased' them in case you have to follow it up in a week's time. Older debtors (three months or more) are usually just as responsive, but two calls might be necessary.

Reappraising your outstanding debtors once a month, getting to know your customers' individual quirks, you will quickly form an opinion as to whether there is cause for concern in any particular camp.

Sometimes it is necessary to send a letter, becoming firmer about your just claim. Many people have a series of three letters which become progressively 'tougher' in tone. Should the third letter, containing suggestions that the matter will be passed on to a debt collector or even the Courts, produce no results then *take* this course of action. The law regards failure to pay for goods ordered as unlawful and, should the matter go to Court, the Court Costs are extracted from the 'delinquent' client along with the money you are owed.

By this time, I'm afraid, the customer has probably long since ceased to be a client of yours.

It is possible, if the client has been declared bankrupt or has liquidated *before* you got your money, you will never be paid. In this case, if you have already paid the VAT proportion of that particular sale, you can claim it back, but you may have to produce proof of the client's demise at some later date. The ensuing letters from the liquidator will be enough for this purpose.

There is now an option open to small businesses whereby, basically, they can opt for one of two VAT accounting systems. The most commonly adopted system is to pay VAT quarterly, at the *end* of the month following that quarter. (To give you sufficient time to calculate the sum due, or reclaimable).

But the other system, called cash accounting, takes into account the fact that your clients might be slow to pay. With this method you calculate the due amount having regard to those invoices which have actually been paid but, on the purchasing side, must only include those purchases you have paid yourself.

All businesses have a bad debt every now and then, and this is something that should be allowed for when structuring your pricing, as a fluctuating overhead, in the same way that all shops build their shoplifting losses into their shelf prices.

The good guys pay for the bad boys!

The foregoing should iron out a few of the wrinkles for you and, before you know it, your professional career should be fully under your control. As a final note of warning, when selecting those clients you wish to 'service', please take into consideration there are certain types of business which are traditionally 'suspect' when it comes to 'playing the game'. Libel laws forbid me to mention those trades in question, but always bear in mind there are some risks which are not worth taking. This is where your own personal judgment comes into its own!

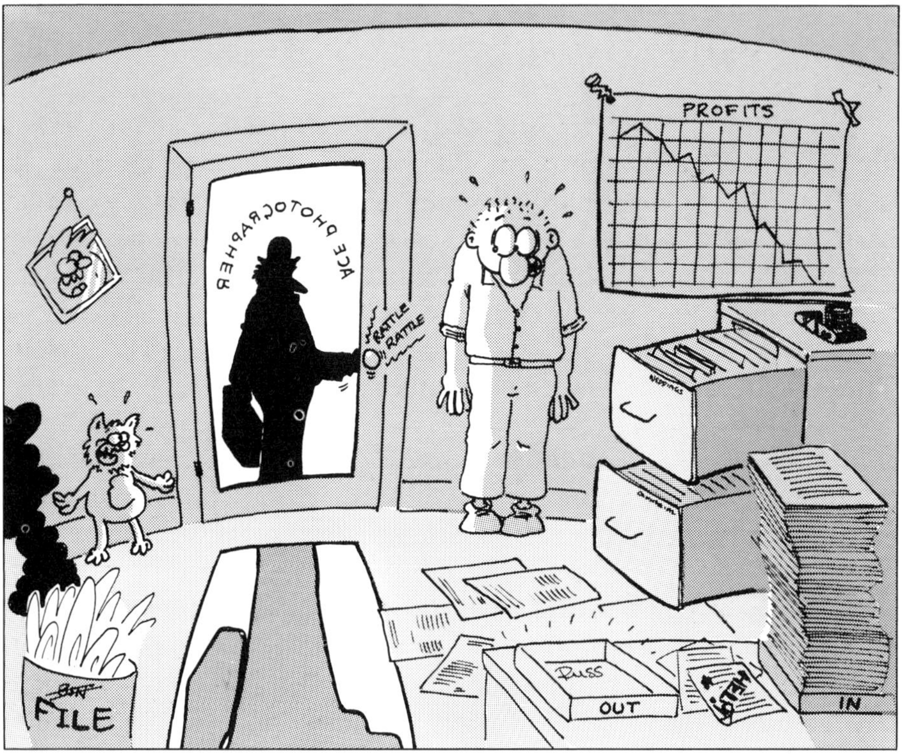

VAT, and all that.

Please do not ignore this chapter. If it was called "How to Get Your Money Back", you would be on the edge of your seat with anticipation – but that's exactly what you can do. To many people, VAT is a dirty word (as is tax of any sort) but the fears most people have about VAT are really quite unfounded. Let me explain.

The object of this book is to show you how you can earn good money and, being VAT registered is, in itself, a way in which business people can reclaim a good proportion of the money they have spent on vital purchases. The general public don't have this privilege, so consider yourself one of the elite.

If you invoice more than £35,000 per annum, you *must* register yourself with the VAT people. You have no choice. Being registered means that all your invoices have to include VAT on the 'bottom line'. If your clients are VAT registered themselves, then for every invoice they receive with VAT included, they can reclaim that VAT back.

Should you be taking portraits and baby pictures, where you are dealing with a general public who cannot reclaim VAT, the decision to register may be tempered by the need to stay competitive. Invoices to the general public are often better received if they don't draw attention to this 'surcharge'. You certainly can't charge a customer VAT if you are not registered, or you might get locked up for your audacity!

If you are turning over less than £35,000 per annum, you can still 'voluntarily' register for VAT and, if you think that your clientele are themselves 'in the VAT club', then it would be desirable from everybodys point of view. If you have doubts, you should apply to your local VAT Office and they would discuss your position with you. It may be that you would benefit from registering, it may not. I have found these VAT people very approachable, and quite helpful. In other words, they don't appear to have an axe to grind and they will show you both sides of any problem, being honest and acting in your interest.

When you do expect to invoice over £35,000 per year (not a large sum by photographers standards) you have to inform the VAT office of that fact, and they will send you a simple form to fill in. Eventually you will be issued with a VAT number. That number has to appear on each invoice you send out. Officially, you can't charge VAT unless you include the number. VAT is a tax surcharge and takes the form of a percentage added onto your own invoice. You are simply collecting money from your clients, to give to the tax-man.

The biggest complaint about VAT is the paperwork involved, and the fact that it has to be done whether you want to or not. But it can work for you in several ways. Let us look at a sample invoice.

You worked for a couple of days, at £300 per day, added £60 worth of materials and processing, travelling expenses came to £45, post

& package was £2.50, and you had lunch out twice at £10 each. These will all be itemised on your invoice and added up at the end of a neat column. That comes to £727.50.

This is your fee for what you have done, but you now have to itemise the VAT. So, the VAT on £727.50 at 18 percent, for instance, is £130.95. Add that on to your bit, and the full invoice value, including VAT, is £858.45. When your client pays your invoice he pays you the full £858.45, even though your work only came to £727.50. Meaning you have been paid £130.95 of the taxman's money which will sit in your bank account gathering interest, until the time comes to declare your VAT, anything up to four months later, depending on what system you have opted for (there is a choice). By the time VAT payment falls due, you could have a few thousand in the bank that doesn't belong to you. It's not a bad idea to keep a separate bank account for VAT payments – one that will gain a good rate of interest for yourself.

There are other benefits. Every invoice you get from your suppliers, such as petrol, meals, colour lab charges, telephone bills, includes VAT. So do many of your other purchases, though some purchases are VAT exempt. But where you pay VAT, you can claim it back if you are VAT registered. So therefore you have to keep careful books, listing all purchases, breaking them down into 'pre-VAT' (nett), VAT content etc. To save you time, the VAT content will often be listed by your suppliers in a breakdown at the foot of each invoice, just like the invoices you send out.

When the VAT is inclusive but not itemised, as it might be for, say, petrol, then you have to calculate the VAT content to claim it back. At 17.5 percent the VAT amount you can claim back on £20 worth of petrol is £2.98. This figure can be arrived at by using a 'VAT fraction'. The method I use is to multiply by 7 and divide by 47. This fraction will vary according to the VAT percentage in operation at the time.

It's wise not to leave your bookkeeping chores for too long, otherwise you'll feel less like doing them than ever. Once a month is about right.

When you have added up your sales invoices, and totalled how much you have collected for the tax-man by way of VAT, you then add up your purchases, not forgetting the VAT content column. THE VAT YOU ACTUALLY PAY THE INLAND REVENUE IS CALCULATED BY SUBTRACTING YOUR 'PURCHASES VAT' FROM YOUR 'SALES VAT'.

If you're doing it right, your sales VAT will be a good deal more than your purchases VAT. Perhaps two or three time larger, depending on your profit margins. That is good! It means you are probably making a profit.

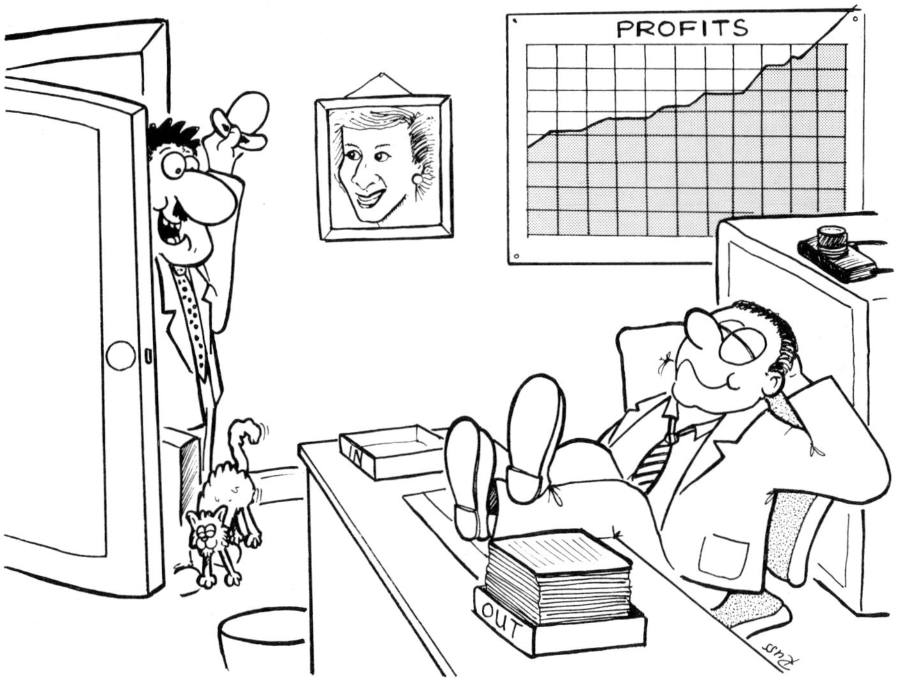

I feel the reason why VAT strikes such horror into careless people's hearts is because they feel they are paying tax out of their own pockets. They are not! They are merely looking after the tax-man's money. When VAT time comes around, and they haven't got the money to pay it, it's because when cheques come in they have forgotten they added 17.5 percent onto their own invoice for the tax-man. Never consider VAT on sales as your own money, and when you add up your monthly sales total (to make you feel good and to give incentive) you add up your Nett figures, that's the bit you've earned.

The bookkeeping side that some people complain about ought to be done anyway. With VAT it just gives you a couple more columns. In a way it forces busy or careless people to make time to keep records, often for their own good.

Banking & Finance.

Handling your Money.
There will be times when money is flowing into your bank account like there is no tomorrow and you will become as blase about thousands of pounds as you might have about much lesser sums before you began your professional career. With this comes a feeling of security and, for some, euphoria. The foolish could be tempted to go on a spending spree.

My advice to them is DON'T !

At least, not yet! Look at your list of creditors, some of whom were instrumental in making that money for you in the first place. They have to be paid, as do the less obvious overheads of telephone, mobile 'phone, car maintenance, etc, and, of course, there will be invoices to pay you may not yet have received. Credit card companies, for instance, or creditors who are slow in reminding you of their dues.

Even after you have consulted your 'outstanding creditors' file and projected ahead so that you know all your forthcoming commitments, you will still be 'fairly well off'. But, have you forgotten anything? Like, for example, the VAT content of the money you have received?

Some of which, after you have done your quarterly VAT return, you will have to hand over to H.M.Customs & Excise. Don't forget you are only collecting and looking after the VAT money for them so that you may deduct your legitimate Purchases VAT from your Sales VAT, then they get the difference!

No doubt, after this short exercise, you will still feel happy about the 'status quo'. It's nice to be rid of debts (for the time being) and to feel solvent.

At this point, you should already have done your bank 'reconciliation' to establish the true balance of your account. To do this you need to note all monies going into the bank (on the 'credit' side), and list all monies leaving your account, via cheques you have signed and Standing Orders or Direct Debits, going out on a monthly, or otherwise regular, basis. The resultant balance figure is the true state of affairs and is far more up-to-date than the final figure on your bank statement. Bank Statements can be sent to you on request, weekly, fortnightly, or at any interval you feel appropriate. I use my bank statements to keep a close check on my *own* records, ticking off each transaction, both on the statement and in my reconciliation book. This way, I watch everything!

Once you have established a system, it takes mere minutes to keep things up-to-date, so long as it is done once every week. The benefits are obvious. You will avoid the possibility of being overdrawn, thus avoiding bank charges but, more importantly, the knowledge that things are under control gives a feeling of security. None of us like nasty surprises and, when you have this total control, you can move money around your bank accounts, shunting funds from a low or no-interest current account into one which gives a good return. I call the account which yields the most interest my 'buffer' account. It is there to protect and insulate me against 'shocks'. It can hold your VAT and your Tax dues, sitting there gathering interest until needed and it can be fed by any overflow from your current account. It may be used for a multitude of things, funding new equipment, buying a car, or maybe taking a working holiday. But don't forget, the real reason for the existence of your 'buffer' fund, apart from earning a higher rate of interest and for paying the Tax-Man, it is your reserve for funding the unforeseen. Like unexpectedly high bills for a major car repair, or paying heavy, on-going expenses should a big job crop up. On an even more pessimistic note, it will tide you over the quiet times should there be any low-turnover months, or should you have a bout of 'flu, or worse!

Peace of mind is a marvellous thing, but some people are prone to worrying unnecessarily. If you fret about the possibility of breaking a leg, insure against it! If you worry about being poor, stop spending money! Or at least slow down. Spending money is easy, of course. We are all experts at it, and it's a fun thing to do, but there are innumerable people queuing up to relieve you of your cash.

Advertising in the Yellow Pages may be a good investment, but, the more widely you advertise, the more you will be inundated by tele-sales people. These can be insurance men, investment brokers, time-share bandits and an army of con-men (and women) who have been skillfully trained to part you from your money, often before you have even earned it. The variety of their wares is almost endless. I have even had 'phone calls from people trying to sell me Kruggerands, or uncut diamonds. These people don't easily take 'No!' for an answer. The first sign of any weakness on your part will be your undoing. Trained to go for the kill should you falter (they call it 'closing'), they won't let you go. Be firm and decisive or every alternate 'phone call you get will be some con-merchant wasting your time and clogging up your most valuable link with customers, your telephone!

Learn it here, not from personal experience! If you are bored or lonely, or simply want to talk to somebody, go out and talk to some little old lady who will appreciate your company and *she* will expect no more than that!

The 'buffer', your nest egg, is there for you, not to be eroded by promises and patter from opportunists whose sole objective is to sell to make their commission. Some people have forgotten the real meaning of 'nest egg'.

An egg, already in a nest, is an encouragement for a hen to lay even more eggs. Your nest egg can become the means whereby you make your next few thousand, and so on. No question about it, money makes money. People with money get the best deals. People without money pay through the nose for most things. If you pay by instalments you can pay as much as the equivalent of double. But pay with cash, and you can usually get discounts.

To Borrow or not!

This business of positive thinking is all very well, you say, but it's a known fact that it is extremely difficult to appear confident and self-assured when you are struggling to keep the wolf from the door. Were you to receive the good news that you had come into a lot of money rather suddenly, your spirits would soar, because the pressure would be off you to provide, proving the feeling of dejection due to lack of work is a psychological one. Naturally, the best way to avoid such pressure is to keep your overheads as low as possible.

If you knew you only had to work for one or two days a week to maintain a certain standard of living and pay your way, anything extra on top of that would be a bonus. And, of course, you would know that the proceeds from such work could be used to enlarge on your professional equipment, or maybe fund a deserved holiday. However, if you have structured your outgoings in such a way that you need to work *four* days a week to break even, then the pressure would be on you to maintain that quota every week of every year, for so long as you have those overheads.

Borrowing from your bank, or from anywhere else, you have to repay the loan with interest, which only puts more pressure upon you. The relief of having sufficient funds after obtaining a loan is short-lived because the reality of the increased overheads will soon bite. Bank interest is an overhead that can quickly get out of hand and, of course, the repayments are always linked to the bank-rate at the time.

Other forms of loans can be even more crippling, with interest rates ranging from 25%, if you are lucky, to 50% or more if you are daft or extremely naive. If you're still not sure what I am getting at, calculate, with the help of your bank manager or somebody equally qualified, how interest rates can drastically affect the real cost of taking out a loan. Borrowing even £2000 has to include interest to fund the people who put the money at your disposal in the first place and, over a period of two or three years, you could be paying back £3000 to £4000!

So how can you avoid such crippling overheads? Usually the problem does not stem from anything outside your control. The most frequent causes of increased overheads can certainly be avoided. All that's needed is to swallow our pride and settle for a car that is practical, buy the Porsche when it can really be afforded. Buy a Hasselblad outfit if you must, but wait until you can *afford* to buy it, maybe in a year or two. Posing is all very well, but there is nothing more humbling than going hungry, or losing faith with your creditors, whilst you are living beyond your means.

On those heady, halcyon days when you feel you are obscenely overpaid for what you do, remember *this*. The days you are productive have to pay for those when you are not, and there must always be some days which cannot be regarded as productive in any way. No matter how busy you might be, at times you will be forced to commit yourself to the desk, or spend time planning for a forthcoming job. This is part of being a professional photographer, so accept those moments as a necessary part of your life because, if you don't, then the whole scene could eventually collapse around you. Making money may be a vital part of our existence, but we do need to get it into perspective.

It has been said, by authorities far more elevated than myself, that one should not feel guilty about making money. It is not a sin, unless we make it dishonestly, or at the expense of those who cannot afford it. Those who choose to criticise the 'lucky opportunist businessman' would never, ever come forward to help should the capitalist's luck run out. The businessman is on his own, he receives support only from his family and a few real friends. Even the support of any salaried staff tends to vaporise when the chips are really down, with few exceptions. This is not meant to sound cynical, or bitter, in any way. It's a fact of life, almost one of the laws of human nature and we should expect nothing more from our fellow-man when it comes to survival.

Whilst we are on the subject of home-truths, let's not forget that the support of the bank would also disappear overnight, should you suffer near-bankruptcy or liquidation. The bank would linger only long enough to claim their rightful spoils. Likewise, the tax-man can never be your friend, his duty is to the State, his employer, his task being to take everything that is proved, or suspected, to be due. It is up to you to disprove it, should you disagree with his assessments. I tell you these horror-stories so that you will not be hurt, or shocked, should the 'chips' ever be down long enough to create dissent amongst your creditors. These are all good enough reasons *not* to feel guilty about making a good profit. Make a profit and you only pay some tax on it. All frightening stuff, but it has to be said. Bury your head in the sand if you will, but if you do then eventually life will overtake you and the consequences will have to be faced.

Despite the foregoing warnings, your daily working life can be fun and that's how it should be. Yet I believe in knowing the full facts, because only then can we face reality. The unknown holds more fears for us than what we fully know and understand. There is always a calming satisfaction in being 'in control', and we cannot feel in control if we choose to ignore certain less-pleasant aspects of our business lives, (nor in our personal lives either, for that matter).

Let us look at another side of the coin for a while, lest we neglect the full picture. Although some of us may think otherwise, photography with its incumbent duties cannot, in my opinion, be considered a 'cushy number', rewarding though it may be. Financially, *and* in a job-satisfaction way, but in my experience it can be physically demanding and not without its stresses. The working hours can be unsociable, to say the least, and done with the proper amount of conscientious effort, you should experience fatigue at the end of your average day. Proof indeed that it is not an easy option. You ought to also experience elation brought on by a feeling of achievement but, in truth, there are few jobs that can compare with photography as a career. Job-satisfaction, creative release, travel, individual challenge, personal achievement and recognition – and, as a bonus, considerable financial rewards. Even bank managers envy us our vocation!

Copyright Advantages.

As a profession, photography enjoys a certain status and some actually envy us our chosen vocation, indicating the genuine regard our profession enjoys. Even "Royals" may pursue the profession without fear of disgrace or demeaning themselves in any way. Could that be said of many professions?

What is it that makes the photographer socially acceptable? Certainly, at best, it is regarded as a fine art. This belief has recently been reinforced by the new Copyright laws which place photography on the same level as painting, music, writing, architecture, etc. Copyright laws mean that authorship of any description is protected from exploitation and abuse. The most recent rulings on the subject have provided us all, amateur and professional alike, with a degree of protection that hitherto was thought impossible. Good news indeed, and the full ramifications have yet to be explored. Now, when we take a photograph, unless we are tied to an employer or have signed a waiver relinquishing our legal rights, the full ownership of that photograph stays with us and our heirs for fifty years after death. Don't fret about the 'death' part of it, simply rejoice in the lifetime of extra revenue that is our right under these new rulings.

Back in the middle of the nineteenth century, when the discovery of photography enabled all and sundry to have a likeness done on Daguerreotype, or similar, the portrait painters of the time were in fear of their livelihoods. To protect their profession, they saw to it that photography was regarded as no more than a copying process, without the need for artiness of any description. Because it was, by comparison, an instant reproduction of a likeness, Royal fine arts got away with it until 1988. I believe we photographers should now make up for lost time!

NOTES

NOTES

CHAPTER NINE.

Contracting-Out and Mark-Up.

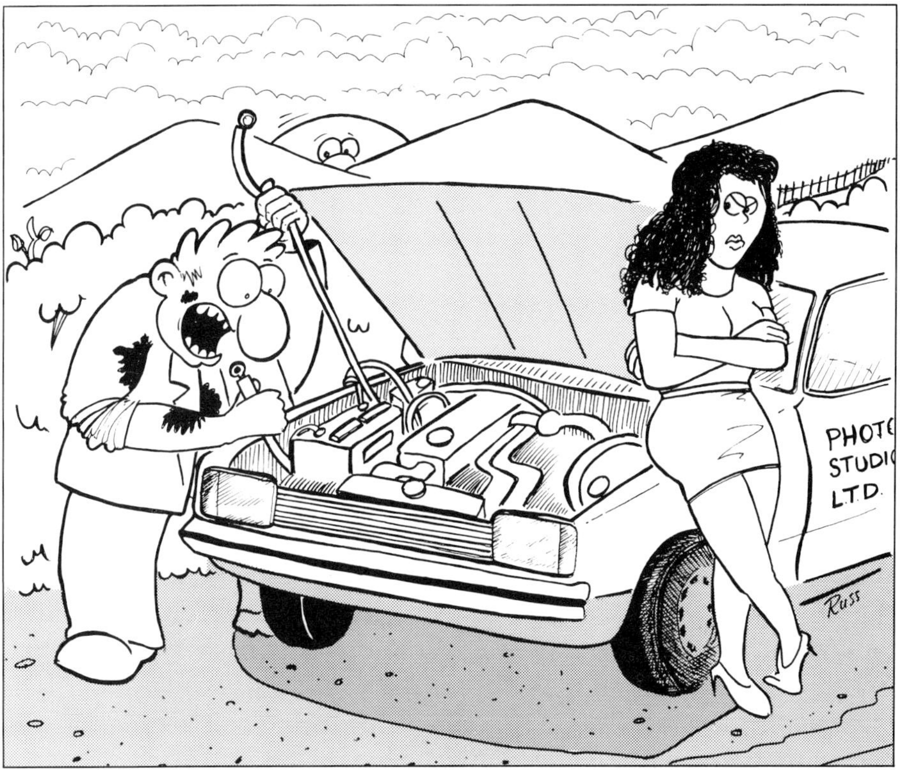

"With a Little Help from your Friends".

We are, first and foremost, photographers, that is our speciality, and what we are quite handsomely paid to do. No matter how gifted we think we are in other fields, it doesn't make good business sense to be a jack-of-all-trades. Yes, it's nice to know how a car works, and some of us like to dabble in electronics for instance, but our time is too valuable to spend it struggling under a car bonnet, or dismantling a video-recorder on the studio floor. So, unless you have 'served your time' as a mechanic earlier on in your career, I suggest you leave the 'de-coke' to the experts. Perhaps they, in turn, will promise not to take photographs for a living.

How can it make sense to service your car yourself if your own hourly rate is almost double that charged by the garage? Furthermore, if you fix your car yourself, you won't be able to give yourself an invoice for the work done, which means you can't enter that expense on your 'purchases' records, nor claim the VAT back. And if, in attempting to change a brake cylinder yourself, you cause further damage, who carries the can? You would then have to obtain another spare part and have grime and grease up to your elbows, crawl under your car once again, cursing as grit drops into your eyes, and you take the skin off your knuckles for the third time. It cannot be worth it.

If you hope to carve a name for yourself as a professional rather than spend your spare time tinkering with a car, there are countless areas where your time can be more profitably spent, such as adding to your photo-library, reading up on new techniques, or planning ahead. The same principle even applies to a good many photography-related jobs as well. The novelty of processing your own films, and printing them, wears off very quickly and, personally, I find it very time-consuming. I would go so far as to say, mostly, it is a tedious, repetitive chore, best left to those who have modern laboratory equipment, and the necessary inclination. Again, as a professional photographer, your time is better spent taking photographs. It is virtually impossible to make more money in the darkroom than you can with your camera. Particularly if you take into account the paper and chemical costs, not to mention tying up an area, designating it as a darkroom with its necessary equipment overheads.

Realistically, there are some of us who would prefer to keep full control of their own darkroom activities and, if you actually enjoy this side of things, then feel free to indulge yourself. But it will probably turn out to be just that. An indulgence. And speaking as businessmen, we can't really afford the time, even though we appear to be saving a little money. Far better to search out one or two professional laboratories, finding out their strengths and weaknesses so that you can contract-out most of your darkroom work. This doesn't have to mean you lose the personal control we were talking about. Most professional laboratories recognise this 'photographers dilemma' and allocate personnel whose sole task it is to satisfy the whims and fancies of us professionals. They will go to some considerable lengths to ensure we remain confident that our precious materials are in capable hands, and it works.

Please don't confuse contracting-out your darkroom chores with laziness. I've experienced what it is like to work eighteen hours a day, seven days a week and, believe me, when you stop working you simply fall asleep and life becomes a drudge! Work and sleep, sleep and work...! I've often slaved through the night in the darkroom after spending a full day taking photographs. A character-building experience, maybe! But how long can anyone keep that up for?

The trick, of course, is to be fully organised, conducting your life in a choreographed manner, where you do your REAL job, leaving the bits you would prefer not to do to others. This way, you will always enjoy taking photographs. That is what we want to achieve, isn't it?

So, just imagine, whilst you are a hundred miles away taking pictures on a gorgeous beach with a bevy of beautiful girls, your radio-phone rings: a minor query from the laboratory technician. At this point you have a choice. Do you tell him where you are and what you are doing? (Are you a sadist, or what?!) Unless you really *are* a sadist, I suggest you keep your secret. Even an out-and-out poseur couldn't be that cruel. However, if he asks you, tell him you are in the Cotswolds, that is kinder. But think to yourself how lucky you are not to be in a darkroom. Thank the poor darkroom technician for his trouble, tell him "Have a nice day", and count your blessings. After all, here you are doing what you do best, and earning money, whilst someone else is doing your processing, which you are going to mark-up by a hundred percent anyway!

Did I hear somebody say "What a rip-off!"? "Some poor sod is 'locked' in a darkroom doing the printing for you whilst you swan around sunning yourself on a beach, and you are marking-up his work by one-hundred percent?".

Well, to be honest, it might not always be a hundred percent – sometimes it's more! It used to be less but I wised up. I found out what certain professional bodies were suggesting their members should charge, and my prices were nothing like theirs. Officially, those professional bodies are not supposed to 'fix' prices these days, because it's against the 'cartel' law. They can only give strong hints to protect photographers from exploitation, (and sometimes from each other). The profession has to 'suggest' its guidelines somehow, otherwise we might end up cutting each others' throats (and we do need to preserve some of our elitism).

To demonstrate this business of mark-up, let's go back to our 'garage' example. When you study their invoice for services rendered, you will likely see the labour content itemised. This is similar to our operating charges and is calculated by taking into account all garage overheads, including the mechanics' wages. Next they should have itemised all materials consumed to do their service properly, plus any extras like brake shoes if they relined the brakes. In common with most service industries, each item consumed or supplied is charged at a profit. In other words, they might mark-up the cost of a set of spark-plugs by maybe fifty percent. This is justified as a handling charge because the plugs have to be ordered and stored and there is also paperwork involved. Most service industries operate this way, though it may not always be noticed if the charges are considered reasonable. Anyone buying a bottle of wine or champagne in a night-club will realise that mark-ups can vary enormously.

In our profession we have similar problems to our garage example, in place of spark-plugs, read 'prints', or materials and processing, even post and packaging, courier, or any 'contract-out' expenses you might have incurred. Everything we buy-in must include some mark-up to cover our overheads and, of course, boost our profits. There is no sin in making a profit, so long as it doesn't appear that you are profiteering.

As I journey through life I keep my eyes open and an ear to the ground and there are many lessons to be learned. For instance, I quickly noticed that my valued clients who are in advertising, or in graphic design, use the mark-up system all the time. They are marking-up my own fees to them by as much as they can get away with. The amount varies from job to job for the following reasons.

We, as photographers, are often at the end of a chain of services, starting with the 'real' customer who initiated the work. Next in line is usually the agent or agency who elected himself, or was chosen, to fulfil the brief. That agency then has to elect various people to carry out a host of duties in order to achieve the desired end result. He might, as a successful agency, have many of the skills already in-house, in the shape of ideas-men, visualisers, lay-out artists and designers, but there are usually many services that are shopped-out to the most suitable people for the job. This can include photographers, specialist artists, lithographic printers and the like. In order that the agent can prepare an overall costing for his own paying client, quotes have to be obtained from each contributor to confirm that they will stay inside the budget allowed.

In practice, when the agency took their client's brief, they probably did a quick mental calculation, and looking at the whole picture of necessary expenses, gave a figure from off the top of their corporate heads. Their figure obviously left plenty of room for a healthy profit margin, and each of the services that would be bought-in each meant a further opportunity to make a bob or two. After all, it is the agency's expertise in choosing the right people, both in their salaried staff and in contract-out services, that will decide the success, or otherwise, of the whole campaign. Each of the elected contributors form a team controlled by an account executive/ co-ordinator, and his (but often *her*) expertise is paramount in the whole exercise. When any service is bought-in a fairly firm price has to be agreed and, in the case of an artist who is quoting for doing a full-perspective water-colour of some architectural development, he has to take into consideration his estimated time for doing it, plus a profit margin to cover all his overheads.

Using hypothetical figures, we will say that the artist considers £400 a fair price. Our agent knows that his own client is from the big City, and is accustomed to City prices. The agent accepts the artist's quote, and he might request written confirmation from the water-colour specialist, along with a firm time for completion. When the work is delivered to our agency, the people are thoroughly impressed. In fact, *so* impressed that they can justify a special price of their own for organising such creative and beautiful work. The price is now being passed on as £1200 pounds, because that is what it is considered to be worth. That is a mark-up of some 300 percent, but justified as fair because it was the skill of the agency, and its employees, who negotiated the figure in the first place. There is a real art in negotiating these days and profit margins, naturally, vary enormously, each transaction judged according to its own circumstances. In a possibly less dramatic way, our own profession is involved in a similar chain of events.

To illustrate this point, there have been occasions when I have met my graphics-designer client outside the entrance to the paying customer's premises, to be told that, for the benefit of this particular client, if the topic came up in the briefing, I charged £500 per day. That being the highest figure he had decided the job would stand. He confessed he had 'sung my praises' to boost a higher fee in order that he might rake-off an extra hundred pound for each day I spent on the photography.

When a media client requests a quote for my services, and his own client is well used to sky-high City prices, I know any figure I give will be marked-up accordingly. We live with this sophisticated form of 'pimping', shrugging our shoulders in the knowledge that we are making our bit and, so long as we are gainfully employed making a profit, why should we care? We are not there to judge the ethics of others if we would do similar things ourselves.

But the lessons to be learned can benefit us all. In knowing the rules of the game, we can make them work for ourselves. If we are shrewd enough to negotiate a special price from the laboratory printing our negatives, a price that gives a ridiculous profit for virtually doing no more than trotting along to the lab, should we feel guilty? Or are we, in turn, simply benefiting from our own skills to negotiate special rates? After all, that could be called private enterprise in action. The degree to which we use this 'art' is, obviously, left to us as individuals but, if you are having a problem coming to terms with it, I'm afraid it is already too late for you to opt out. In buying this book, you are at the end of a chain where the mark-up is normally 100 percent. Jewellry is the same, and some items of clothing in the shops may have originated in Taiwan, made by children for a pittance; and each step of its way to you means a very healthy profit, and a living, for someone else. There may be four or more middle-men before a purchase is made. An object with a basic value of a few pence can ultimately sell for many pounds. Believe me, it's true. Thus is the way of the world, you can't beat them, so why not join them?

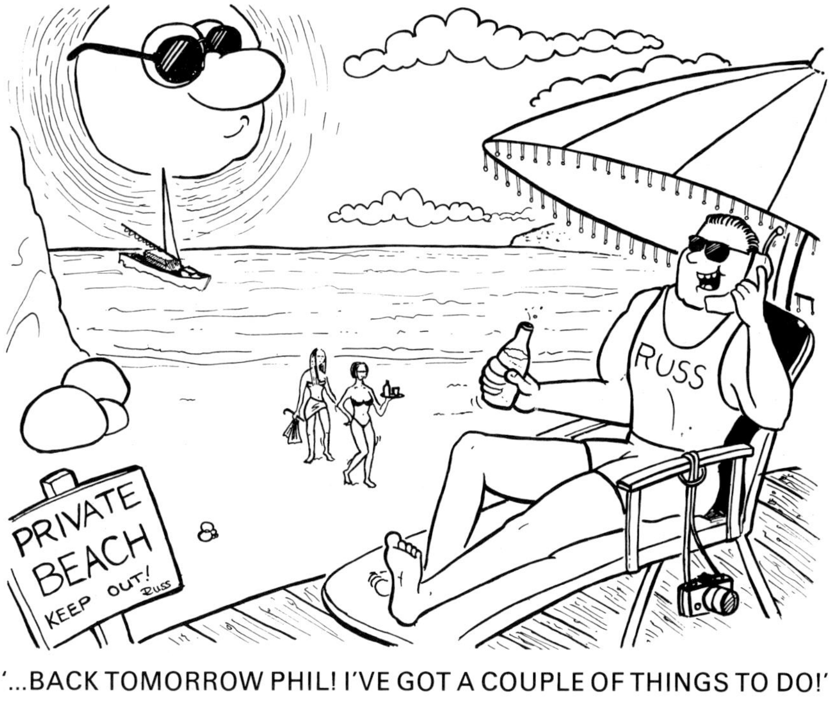

'...BACK TOMORROW PHIL! I'VE GOT A COUPLE OF THINGS TO DO!'

As ever, there is something you can do to ease your conscience! Few of us find ourselves in a position to do anything to put the world right, however hard we might try, regardless of how high-principled we may be; but we can do something, as individuals, to equalise the state of affairs. We can off-set our profits, to some extent, by giving freely to charity. We make good money and are in a position to make that money work for us in so many ways. It might be a simple pledge, personally to donate the gathering interest from one bank account towards a 'pet' charity. Or, if one of your client's *is* a charity, to do some work for them and not charge. The choices are yours; but there is a school of philosophy that says "For every pound given away with a good heart, you will be rewarded two or three fold, somehow or other". I know it works, and it's called the law of natural returns.

Lord Nuffield, industrialist and famous benefactor extraordinaire, was a prime example of this philosophy. How could he have done such fine charitable works if he had not made money? His legacy lives on today!

And, don't forget, charitable donations are tax-allowable!

CHAPTER TEN.

Creative Travelling.

It's all very well to glibly talk about creativity, but how do we go about getting it? We recognise creative work when we see it, and can acknowledge creative talent, but how can we turn our own tap on? Plainly, it's one of those things that's easier said than done and to some of us it doesn't come easy. I would include myself in that category but I've learned a few tricks to rectify the situation. If we follow a few pointers, the whole idea of creativity starts to become clear.

Because you can't bottle it, or buy it, we recognise it as one of those intangibles, like 'love'. We can't see creativity, only the effect of it. No doubt, to some of us, it comes easy and we wonder if, like talent, you are either born with it or you are not. However, if we believed that then, for the majority of us, life would be hopeless. We would be doomed from the start. And rightly we cannot accept such a thing, for to do so is unthinkable.

Anybody who doubts we all have a latent ability to be creative should look at history where there are so many lessons to be learned. Even prehistoric man felt within himself a need to make his cave-paintings. These may have been prompted by semi-religious belief that, by doing them, he would improve his hunting chances. Regardless of his motives he was able to stylise his artistic efforts to a point where he wasn't just copying from nature, but developing 'form' and 'line' until, with a few simple strokes, he could depict an antelope in a way that is recognised as truly artistic, even today. It's amazing how, in those times of unimaginable hardship and day to day survival, man still found a need to be creative.

We are not born creative. Babies don't sing, or write poetry, or paint pictures. These gifts are born within us all, locked in the complexity of our brains, but don't manifest themselves until we have acquired some experience of life. The experience of living provides the necessary stimulation to provoke our creativity and such stimulation is around us all the time we are growing up, continuing for the rest of our lives.

To lose a love, or to gain one, has prompted man for many centuries to creativity of one sort or another.

Patriotism, another strong emotion, spurs some people on, as does religion, jealousy, ambition, pride and a host of strong, emotive feelings.

Michelangelo, when he painted the Sistine Chapel, had to be motivated. Perhaps in his case it was a mixture of religious fervour, duty, pride, stubbornness, or the persuasion of money. (He already had the technical ability). Whatever his motives, we cannot doubt the brilliance of his work which survives today as a monument to man's creative resourcefulness. We all have that same creative ability within us, we just need to know which buttons to press to make it all work.

But perhaps therein lies the problem for many of us. There is such a thing as 'trying too hard': we can find ourselves suffering from something called 'purpose tremors'. In other words, in striving to succeed, we involuntarily trigger within ourselves an anxiety that can block our creative channels. Far better to cultivate a relaxed attitude on the subject, where we allow our auto-pilot mechanism to work for us. It has long been accepted that the human species has its own goal-seeking device. It has nothing to do with willpower, or positive-thinking, but is simply our own personal guidance system that, even left to its own devices, will solve problems for us while we are doing something else, even whilst we sleep. Don't ask me exactly how it works. All I know is that it does!

Let's look at this business of 'making pictures' for a moment. We must accept, here and now, that there is nothing 'magical' about a camera. Even though it may be a clever piece of modern technology, any 'thinking' it does is limited to routine things, such as calculating exposure, counting frames and maybe focussing. In fact, all the mundane stuff, should we not care to take full manual control ourselves.

The way technology has gone in the past decade we could wander around snapping pictures willy-nilly all day, of a dozen different subjects, and we could easily end up with many rolls of perfectly-exposed, critically-sharp photographs. They might, of course, only be a record of where we pointed the camera. With today's cameras you can get exactly what you see, but no amount of "taking photographs" will create fine pictures. Good pictures are not 'made' in the camera, but in the mind. This is why a £1000 camera in the hands of the unthinking can only take 'snaps'. By the same token, a bottom of the range point-and-squirt compact camera can produce exhibition results in the hands of a true master.

So, we are agreed! It's the operator, not the equipment, which makes all the difference. The equipment's necessary level of refinement and excellence need only be decided by the answering of two questions. 1) What facilities do we need on the camera and, 2) how far do we need to go to satisfy our self-image, or that of our esteemed clients who expect us to use a 'professional' camera?

The choice in the market-place is extensive, with perhaps a half-dozen leading manufacturers producing worthwhile system cameras, each with a phenomenal range of lenses and accessories to suit every need. Our needs today may not be the same next month, or next year, so the final choice is very much a personal thing.

Taking great pictures has never been easier than it is now. We no longer have to worry about the technology of such things as correct exposure, so we can concentrate on technique. For me that was a great day dawning – when I finally realised the new-found freedom I had been handed. It took quite a while to adjust to this new world, after decades of developing my own system of operating, my first fears were those of mistrust. Learning to put my faith in the silicon chip didn't come easy at first.

Getting 'In the Mood'.
Quite often the difference between achieving moderate or passable results, and producing an exceptional job, is decided before you actually make a single exposure. Whether you are taking studio still-life, action shots involving people, outdoor architectural or, in fact, any picture of any nature, the following principles are of great importance.

No matter what your subject, the final results are usually decided when you start to plan just how you will set about the job. You must 'get into' the right frame of mind and mood and this involves following a fairly simple set of rules anyone can follow. To jump straight in and click away aimlessly, hoping to somehow or other get the desired results, is not the way it's done. You might, by accident or good fortune, or by sheer volume of film consumed, end up with a few decent shots, but this can be put down to luck rather than good judgment or planning.

For a set of pictures to be successful, they have to meet the following criteria:

1) To satisfy the needs of the end-user, the client, when perhaps even the client doesn't know what his true objectives are.
2) Satisfy yourself, not just in sharpness, exposure and presentation, but you should feel proud, rather than ashamed, to hand the photographs over to your customer, and certainly feel no guilt when giving him the invoice for your work.
3) To be as original as possible. Tackle any job in the usual fashion by all means but, by varying your choice of lens or viewpoint, lighting etc., not only will you gain experience along the way, but you will start to break new ground; keeping your personal standards high, constantly striving for excellence.

Any thinking photographer worth his salt will feel, after the event, that he, or she, could have done something more to have achieved even better results. This is normal, and desirable. Clients will appreciate your efforts, not simply in trying to be innovative in a creative sense, but in demonstrating your caring attitude. You are employed to produce results that work and you must be perceived by them in this light. Effort on your part will be met and received as caring. If you succeed in satisfying these important criteria, then you are halfway there. To be thought of as good is an ongoing battle. When it works the world truly does beat a path to your door. Whether the incentive to achieve this goal is prompted by money, or by a strong desire to be considered "good", doesn't matter too much. The end results are one and the same and go hand in hand.

Using this code of practice I have 'stolen' clients from other photographers. But make no mistake about it, as soon as you get too complacent, or stop trying quite so hard, the system is reversed – clients can slip away one by one. Lost by default. Your default. So the watchword is CARING.

Having started the snowball rolling, you then have to maintain the momentum or one day it will stop abruptly soon after you stopped trying your best.

Achievement, and receiving accolades, is a great spur to your creative efforts and, for some, is almost payment enough in itself. Just for kicks you might do some jobs for nothing but, being practical, we put a fee on such talents. Any fee should correspond to the value of increased kudos and image-in-the-market-place your pictures will give your client. This is one reason why costing-out your efforts is such a personal headache. If we all produced excellence every time there would be less of a problem. We certainly must be seen to be trying our best on every occasion.

People pay quite gladly for results that work. It's very important to come across as a caring, thoughtful, efficient operator, whose sole objective is to promote a client's product in the best possible light. To appear as though you will continue to strive for even greater goals on his behalf can only be met with satisfaction from the client. It's your job to make your client look good and, it will make you look good in the process. If you succeed in this, then he won't be able to wait to give you more work, to weave your magic for him yet again.

This is all very well but, now we know how the system works, how do we set about it? We all want satisfied clients! We all want to be thought of as "good"! To be thought of as experts! How do we set about this when we have never done it before, when we don't feel in the least bit creative, and can't seem to find the magic button to set our creative juices flowing? We can be our own worst critics but, when it all starts to flow, there is such an almighty 'buzz' that some have likened it to being 'high' on magic mushrooms! Because it is *real* the effect is even better, and not induced by artificial means that wane when the chemicals wear off. So, how do we do it, convincingly and with results?

First step; caring enough. You've got to want to succeed for your clients sake first; then for yourself. There is your motivation! The money flows later, almost automatically. Get into your subject. Think about it carefully. If you have been asked to photograph a supermarket, find your client's requirements. Perhaps he wants to show the magnificent architecture, or maybe how happy the shopping customers are just to be there. Does he want a family slant? We should look at the project in question before deciding the best viewpoints – even before picking up our camera. Decide on possible lens choice and perspective, and how these can help us towards a certain effect. We think about filters, special lighting at certain times of day or night, and consider all the different ways in which we can bring out the character and 'feel' of the place. And this is the magic keyword. We will start to 'feel' the place, as we drink in our subject, understanding the moods of the architecture, and how it works with the interaction of people. That is the essence of a successful building, it's interaction with people. The reason for the architectural effort in the first place was to design for use by people. And when we consider the scale of one portion or element to another, the effect of one lighting mood in contrast to another, we then start to feel we can begin to understand why we are there at all. In our appreciation, we start to identify with the architect, the builder, with history even. Our senses, if we allow them the indulgence, will start to take on their own creativity, inspired by the presence of all that's around us.

We may be in the modern dream of the Docklands Project, or wandering around Norwich, with its cathedral and back streets merging with new precincts. Whatever we are doing, if we take the time to try and get into the mood of the subject or place, we cannot fail to be inspired by such strong external stimulus, and our own creative urges will then be fed as long as we wish. This is caring; and, with the caring, comes the emotion that enables us to be creative. Taking the trouble to be more than 'just another photographer', and enjoying the "buzz" that feeds us in our work.

A poet could be inspired by a sunset or a strong emotion. A musician and composer can be inspired by the Seasons or by the movement of a deer-fawn. A writer is driven to creativity in an effort to put feelings into words. So, why should we photographers be any different? Naturally, we do our creating all the better for feeling our response to outside stimulus. Such involvement is part of the thinking-photographer's way of life, especially if he wishes to interpret, and achieve, in a creative sense.

Not all of us can easily identify with the philosophy of the previous paragraphs, that is accepted. It certainly helps to have a sense of awareness of all around us, wherever we may be, but this can quite easily be cultivated.

No matter where we are, at home or abroad, in a factory or lost on a moor, we can't help but feel the atmosphere and sensations around us. When we stand on a hilltop we surely wonder how many thousands of people from bygone times stood at that same spot surveying the same view. When we pick up a baby, don't we marvel at the miracle of new life (before it wets on us!)? Doesn't the unique smell of baby-skin stay with us forever? And so, to a lesser or greater degree, we experience our surroundings, forming opinions, translating those stimuli into poetry, pictures and prose. If you find that odd, remember this; we can be odd if we want to! Some say this is expected of us photographers and we should not apologise for it. Being thought odd or eccentric is certainly better than being boring.

Pictures in Your Head?

We will assume, for this exercise, we already have our technical ability. In other words, we can take photographs. Then we shall imagine a hypothetical assignment of, say, photographing a person using a computer. This is a task that crops up with some regularity, so it could prove useful for the future. I would bet that your mind has already conjured up a mental picture, probably based upon a scene that you have already seen somewhere. You might have lots of images flashing through you mind, again, based on your experiences or memories. Perhaps you have photographed this one before, and you can visualise the results of that instance. I would suggest that, in the space of a few seconds, your brain sifted through the equivalent of a few million megabytes of memory to pop up with your mental picture and, if it failed to find anything relating to a person using a computer, it would quickly fabricate a picture for you, based on a computer that you have seen, and with any person you care to visualise. We will visualise a young woman. You imagine the hair colour, face shape, clothes etc. Isn't this visualisation a marvellous thing? Forget the detailed features or you will become side-tracked. At our computer we have a model's dummy. She isn't smiling, or moving. She can't! You move her by visualisation. So far, the above exercise has taken less than five seconds. It took you much longer to read it.

There you are, armed with experiences you didn't know you had in you; and such an inventive mind. In fact, it's childs play. Literally.

Now, we are in a real situation, if you like. Real computer, real live person, and you have the necessary equipment with you. Camera, tripod, and some form of lighting, plus various bits and pieces of photographers' paraphernalia, maybe umbrellas, light-meter, flash-gun/s, etc.

Don't pick up your camera yet, you don't need it until you are ready. The camera is simply a "means whereby you capture your visualised picture". You know how to use it, but you are 'taking pictures' with your mind's eye at the moment.

Scan through your memory banks again for variations on a theme. You are only going to take one picture, but if you wish, you can take several differing exposures. I know I would.

Using your marvellous visualisation trick you can, without even moving from the spot you are standing on, rotate your viewpoint around your subject, zoom in, zoom out, change 'lenses', move up or down, and balance in your mind's eye the sort of lighting you would like to try. You want only one shot, because that is all you need. There are possibly thousands of permutations of angle choice, but you are capable of picking just one – the best one. You are in charge, your brain and you. Revel in the power, because that is real as well. Now you are creating. Feel 'the force', and relax!

Your picture can be composed to fit almost any shape you require, and there is no law that says "show the whole computer", unless the client has specifically directed it. You coolly pick your optimum angle, with the confidence of one that has been this way before (and in your mind you have), then consider the lighting. It's fluorescent at the moment, apart from the screen monitor. Kill the fluorescent, calculate the screen-only exposure and decide upon soft side-light with flash off a brolly, keeping any light off the screen. Lighting permutations are seemingly endless but, master of the situation, you make your decision, with some variations, and it's in the bag.

You know there are thirty thousand ways of skinning a cat, this has been only one of them! Now, based on what you have just done, for real or in your imagination (there is no difference), do it all again; differently. Tackle every problem with enthusiasm, intentionally throwing your own spanners in the works, just to keep you and your brain alert. Once you have done that a few times you will be ready for some advanced stuff. This time choose another original angle, and light it as you have never seen it done before. Be unconventional. You have already done the job to your satisfaction, so now you can experiment; and possibly break new ground. Back-lighting, mix light-sources, different filter-gels. Or play around in the darkroom later, to create your own original, visualised composition. There is no limit to your creative ability. Your results will soon prove this.

Being of an inquisitive nature, I try to find out what makes people tick. As part of my search for the "meaning of life" I am always observing and occasionally, when the right moment presents itself, I ask people some fairly pointed questions. In our line of work it is common-place to meet some very talented, and sometimes famous, people.

For instance, amongst the most clever graphic designers I know is one who consistently sits on top of the creative pile. He is acclaimed throughout the United Kingdom as being simply one of the best. To get there he naturally had to work hard and, by his own admission, staying there at the top is even harder. It requires constant monitoring of what is going on in the design world, keeping pace with fashions in typefaces, new computer-technology, special papers and processes – the list is frightening. But, in common with most honest graphic designers, he relies quite heavily on what is known as "source" books. Sometimes when he is looking for inspiration or reference he will look through someone else's work. It may be to do with architecture, natural history, sport, or just about anything you care to mention.

He also studies what other people are doing in his field or akin to it. What he does, in effect, is add to his already extensive knowledge, taking bits from here and there, maybe modifying it with a touch of classical design, until all the ideas condense into a new way of looking at his problem-subject. Where is the sin in that? I said earlier that we can learn a great deal from history, and pure fashion is a prime example of this principle.

In the 50's a cult (so-called) singer named Tom Lehrer penned a song with the words, "Plagiarise, let no one else's work evade your eyes. But always be sure to call it 'research'!"

So, when you feel you require just a little bit of creative prompting, why not take in an exhibition of other people's work. Read a book, look back through the classics in photographic art, or study a catalogue of library shots. Therein lies a world of inspiration. Who knows, perhaps one day in the not-too-distant future some young would-be professional will be getting his inspiration from *your* work.

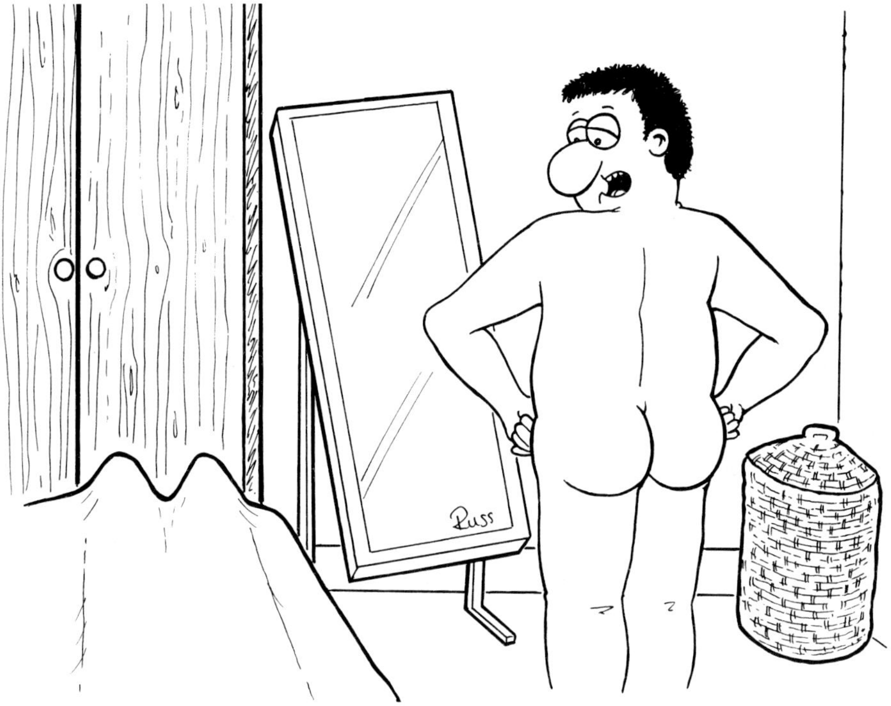

'YOU KNOW, I STILL CAN'T FIND MY CREATIVE BUTTON!'

The Creative Traveller.

If you are the sort of person who prefers not to move out of the area where you are based, you will indeed become provincial in every way. Yes, travel does broaden the mind, but there is more to it than that alone!

I would suggest that travelling, for whatever reason, is one of the more important keys to your success. Even if you don't own your own vehicle it is still possible to be two hundred miles away from home by lunchtime. You can buy a travel ticket which will enable you to use a variety of modes of transport for the duration of that day, or maybe longer and this can work out quite inexpensive.

"So why should I want to travel?", you might say. Well, we all get such a tremendous stimulus from any new environment, and often get the necessary inspiration to see, and create, new pictures. I have noticed, in our own back-yards, we tend not to see those things that a visitor might. Likewise, when I'm in a new place I positively vibrate with all that is new around me, seeing picture-opportunities at every twist and turn.

A senior lecturer friend of mine told me that he was planning a holiday to New York, going on his own. Naturally I asked "Why New York?", and immediately thought that the so-called 'Big Apple' was the last place I should take a holiday; until he explained further. He wanted to go for the atmosphere, the action, the stimulation! This was very much in contrast to the class-room where he spends much of his working life. He said he was particularly interested in the graffiti on the subways and, "The whole of life was there!". I couldn't argue with that, although I would rather volunteer to catch Scud missiles in the Middle East with my bare hands than run the gauntlet of even a one-mile trip on the New York subway! However, he had made his mind up, combining the subway attraction with a visit to see some old friends. I advised him to see his old friends first! He spent a whole day disguising his beloved Nikon as a useless lump of waterproofed black tape, leaving just enough gaps to operate the controls – the desired effect being to make his precious camera look like a worthless lump of junk. A necessary precaution if he intended to travel in the infamous 'underground'.

Surprisingly, I did see him again, and his camera. The two of them came back with some memorable pictures and his experiences were to keep him stimulated until his next sortie, to God knows where! But he knows that travelling with a camera can never be boring!

In the same vein, I have recently acquired a book on Oxford entitled "Inspired Images", a view of the city by a New Zealander who was certainly inspired by what he saw there. The collection of colour photographs he made, in only two years of discovery, are testimony to that fact. I doubt if it could be equalled by a native of the rather special city. Not being prejudiced, by familiarity and habit, his mind had been stirred by a fresh way of seeing the architecture, the seasonal moods of the city, and the people who are the very essence of any place. His name is Jon Davison and, although I have never met him, it is apparent from his collection of images that he understands the subtle nuances of natural light, and how the patient and observant can build a valuable stock-image library. Given the motivation, and the eyes to see what is already there!

I recently read that the esteemed naturalist and anthropologist, Sir David Attenborough, would rather be in a cave up to his waist in bat-dung than stuck in a boring, though executive, office. Anybody who has been even a few hundred yards downwind of a genuine bat-cave will get the message. For him, travelling to new and challenging places is the life-blood of his very existence. Having experienced it, he would not have it any other way.

New people, and places, give us the same fascination which a child on holiday experiences. All good vibes for creating new pictures. Stimulus is everything, even to a seasoned veteran. When I recently encountered the new developments on East London's Isle of Dogs I felt as a child would at Disneyland. Not knowing which way to turn first, surrounded by this plethora of modern day architectural development. The juxtaposition of water and buildings as in Venice; the successful marrying of the traditional with the new!

I only had time for two hours photography before rushing off to another site, a modern airport, and yet another type of stimulus, encountering an East End wedding on the way. A long day with lots to do, starting at sunrise and not returning until after dark. Sixteen sites photographed ranging from an industrial and retail park to the operation of the Woolwich Ferry. At the outset a seemingly impossible list of things to do and, thanks to careful planning and a fine day weather-wise, a successful conclusion with over three-hundred miles on the clock and, I must admit, a feeling of achievement. Something we must not ignore.

Achievement, no matter how trivial, is a very important part of everybody's working life and photographers have the opportunity more than most to experience it. If you're not the worrying sort, and you are reasonably confident in yourself and your equipment, you honestly don't have to wait until you have processed your film to feel it. You know the moment the shutter is released that you have something worthwhile, and each newly captured image adds to that feeling of achievement. You might even get 'high' on the feeling, or maybe get euphoric on occasions.

If you are a worrier then gradually, after the event, self-doubt might creep in as you become concerned that you really *have* captured what you saw. In other words, will your pictures 'come out'? Have you simply been carried away by the excitement of the occasion? In these circumstances the trick is not to dwell upon it. Simply carry on seeing new pictures and trusting to the law of averages. When you eventually see your successes, and have learned from your few minor disappointments, you will begin to enjoy your work without worrying. What you are doing, in actual fact, is replacing any negative feelings with positive ones. Never dwell on even the smallest failure. Learn from it and only look eagerly forward, remembering only your successes!

Work quickly in bursts of energy, then more slowly when the occasion requires it, with relaxed 'thinking and seeing' periods in between. Don't be frightened to use automatic cameras, those that have motor-wind and built-in exposure meters free you from those cluttering calculations. Know when to 'plus' or 'minus' the exposure for effect, or even use a camera that automatically brackets the exposure for you. You will then enjoy the freedom to concentrate on seeing pictures.

There is another spin-off advantage for the travelling photographer. And it comes under the heading of 'image making'. We have discussed your positive feedback due to the feeling of achievement, and with it will come a true aura of success. No matter how small that achievement, it has the vital effect of replacing any latent negative feelings you may be harbouring. Each little success will add to an eventual store of successes and that will change your whole attitude and give you confidence. Your very demeanour will change, as surely as if you had been dressed by the smartest fashion house in Europe. You will feel better and emanate confidence. And others will see it too. In your manner, attitude and body language. "This is no provincial hick! Here is a worldly craftsman who has achieved, and who travels in his work and enjoys life!". You feel it, and believe it! "His own master but a slave to the cause of striving for his art and profession. A perfectionist who regards each new day as a challenge to go on to better things. Fully armed with many past successes under his belt, and who is not afraid of conquering new territory."

Quiet confidence quickly replaces any temporary feelings of conceit or pomposity. You *are* an achiever! Breaking new ground and continually adding to your experience. Expect this state of affairs to last you a lifetime. Never be completely satisfied with yourself, however competent you might appear to others, this is life. The striving for perfection that always eludes us as we lift our standards higher, our goals moved further ahead at each milestone reached.

One happy outcome of this philosophy is an increase in your earning power. The worldly photographer commands higher fees than the run-of-the-mill operator, and he deserves them. Bailey (who needs to ask "Who?") knows his worth! After all, he sets the scene himself. His fame was skillfully engineered by Bailey, taking advantage of the market that wanted him to perform his art. Those who wanted Bailey had to join the queue, for there was only one Bailey and, because one man can only do so much, his fees were governed by supply and demand. Bailey, if motivated, will go anywhere in the world. His self-motivation in a particular field is paramount, before any fees are discussed, along with any fringe benefits. He calls the tune. Then, in common with us lesser mortals, we new-achievers, he still has to produce the goods. He has to plan, visualise and thrash out the foreseeable problems and tackle ongoing ones, just as any professional worth his salt might. His problems are the same as ours. For "Bailey" read "Duffy, Donovan", and many more too numerous to mention.

The principle remains the same.

Your Privileged Position.

Many great pictures are achieved as a result of a person finding themselves in a privileged position. A good example of this is the many hundreds of stunning photographs which have been taken in space, or on 'space-walks'. The photographers in question were not professionals, in the true sense of the word, even though they had some training as part of their preparatory studies. But how can we doubt the significance and impact of their results? Naturally, we don't get to see their failures, but even that wouldn't detract from the beauty of "Earth-rise from the Moon". If I'm envious of anybody, it's only of those courageous astronauts who took such pictures, because they make my own aerial photographs seem so insignificant. Certainly, as professionals, we all have our privileged moments and, although we might be blase about some of the people we meet, places we go, and experiences we have, we should never take those opportunities for granted.

We may never go to the moon but, compared to most people, we have such great opportunities to go to some amazing places that we really shouldn't waste those 'photo-opportunities'. Next time you are going somewhere special, why not telephone a few photo libraries and ask if they could use anything related to that particular area? Start making a list of those libraries now, because that's a positive thing to do!

Before you know where you are they could be the ones ringing *you*!

CHAPTER ELEVEN.

Weddings and Wedding Day Nerves.

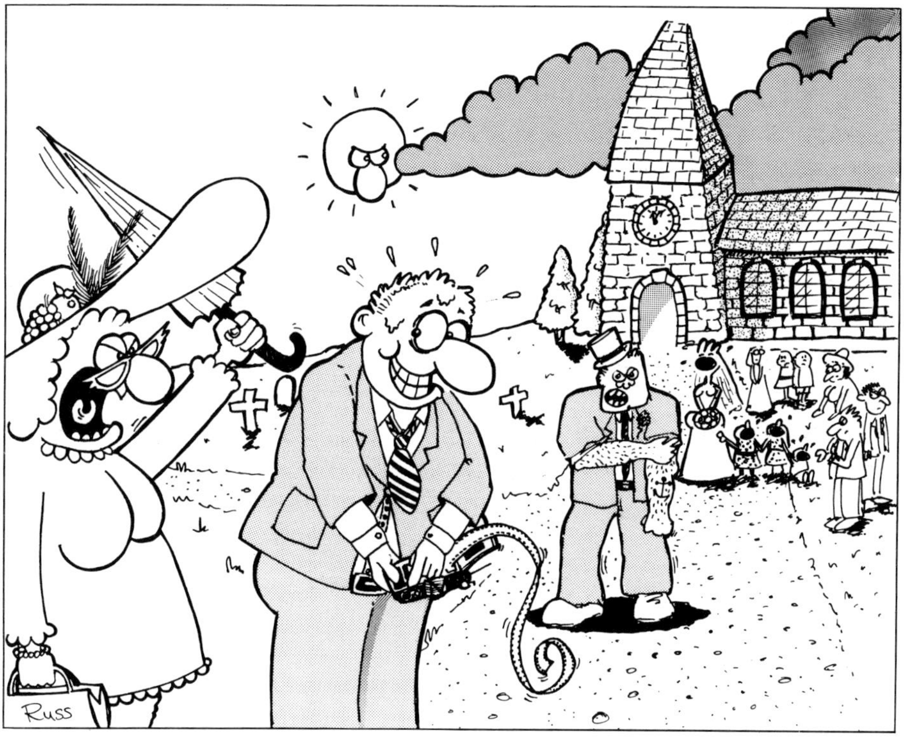

Wedding Day Nerves.

Often, after lectures, students of all ages have come to see me about their own individual problems, a practise I have always encouraged. They have many questions, some of which they would rather not disclose to others in the class for fear of embarrassment. It's at times like these that I have learned so much about the many difficulties facing students of photography but, though feedback is important to help structure future talks and teaching strategies, I have learned of the fears and phobias of otherwise-confident would-be professionals. Indeed, it was my concern for fellow-photographers and their problems that prompted this book in the first place.

Questions and queries were various but fear of failing, particularly at weddings, was perhaps the most universal.

At first this came as a surprise to me. Why should a grown man lie awake at nights worrying over 'doing a wedding'? And that same dread frequently causes strong men to visibly shake at the thought of doing any photographic job which could not easily be taken again. Weddings are certainly a favourite nerve-rattler, with photographing famous people, or even children, close runners up. If such a seemingly routine exercise could give them palpitations, how would they cope with photographing Royalty, or a really awe-inspiring event?

To help me understand the 'fear of failing' syndrome, I looked back at my own experiences and did some lateral thinking. The fear of failing applies to many human situations and is probably at its worst when failing has major consequences, such as one would encounter at an important job-interview, or making an after-dinner speech before hundreds of people. I delved into my own past history first to analyse the problem.

The Problem.

I first met the phobia as a late-teenager in the Royal Air Force, and wondered why I always got the special-visit-by-top-brass jobs. I must admit I enjoyed having the adrenalin flowing in those days and wandering around taking photographs of Group Captains and Air Commodores (and the occasional Chief of NATO) was a better alternative to standing to attention on parade for hours on end in all weathers. It all seemed routine to me, until one day I heard that, whenever I was away 'on leave', the other men in the photographic section used to draw straws to see which unlucky blighter would be standing out like a sore thumb in front of hundreds of troops all stood to attention, whilst Generals and Air Vice Marshalls made their inspections. I deduced it wasn't so much a case of courage on my part but probably ignorance, and a wrong attitude, on theirs.

Weddings, Royalty or ceremonial events, the problems are the same. The official photographer at all such events cannot help being in the spotlight himself to some degree and, to make matters worse, people are relying on you to get results, no matter what the conditions. The pressure's on you. You've got to put up with being 'noticed' and, on top of all that, you are very conscious that you mustn't fumble or look incompetent whilst you change films, focus, take light readings etc, as you try to look cool and efficient and generally get it 'in the bag'. With the foregoing in mind I decided it would be more revealing to look at why certain people *don't* suffer from nerves in this way. If you have confidence in your equipment and your ability to use it, that only leaves your state of mind and your approach to the task in question. Fear has to be put into perspective to rid you of this bogey-man forever. Let us look at one of the worst imaginable scenarios to see where we could go wrong.

The Nightmare!

Maybe you've just started photographing a classy wedding and notice that one of the guests is using a camera costing three times as much as your own. From that moment on you are on the defensive, because it has undermined your confidence slightly and you feel that you may be perceived by others as less than adequate. The trouble is, as you no doubt already know, the moment you feel a little uncertain about something, the nagging doubts set in, and insecurity breeds more doubts and errors.

You're only half-way through your second roll of film and you notice your light-meter is set on the wrong film speed. How long has it been set like that? Or you're using flash and discover the shutter is set to one two-fiftieth of a second with a focal plane shutter that doesn't fully synchronise at speeds above one sixtieth! When did that happen? If you have possibly done that, what else have you done wrong? You are supposed to be taking colour negatives, but you *could* have loaded that roll of Ektachrome you had in your bag; its empty wrapper is still lying there! Did you put film in at all!!?? If you did perhaps it's not winding on!!

And all this whilst you're trying to be creative!

A cold sweat breaks out all over your body as you assess the terrible possibilities in one thousandth of a second – or less. Being deep down a very practical person, you reason that there's nothing to be gained from worrying, but there is nothing you can do to stop it!

You were determined to do a good job and maybe enter that totally gorgeous bride in the "Totally Gorgeous Bride Competition". Now you'll consider yourself luckier than the bridegroom if you get any results at all!

Why is the bride's mother looking agitatedly in your direction? Can she sense your predicament? Maybe she's only looking daggers at an unwelcome relative. You'd like to philosophise about the lives of intrigue surrounding such occasions, but all you want is for this purgatory to end. What you'd really like to do is go back home for a lie-down, then put the clock back so you can do it all again, properly this time! Where did you go wrong!?

The Seeds were Sown.
You went wrong weeks ago. Remember when you took that all-important first booking, and went to meet the bride-to-be and her family? Everything was still alright at that point. Then on the way home the feeling of elation was replaced by self-doubts, which grew over the next few days until you could think of nothing else. When you met friends, the forthcoming wedding soon came into the conversation. As you lay in bed at nights your fears would not leave you alone. And when morning came, there it was again. Anticipation was now trepidation! Eventually, of course, the happy day arrived and you consoled yourself it would soon all be history.

Many of us can identify with the foregoing drama. I know I can! Some of us could maybe confess to worse terrors. But wouldn't it be nice to avoid the trauma altogether, no matter how important the event?

If you were told you could easily cope with a society wedding, with every conceivable 'posy' extra (including the wedding breakfast being held at the Hilton Hotel), you may doubt this. Soon you will not!!

The Treatment.

You know how to get sharp, properly exposed pictures. You've done it many times, and not by accident. So you must now become totally familiar with all your equipment, including films, with their various limitations and attributes. You can operate your camera blindfolded, and change lenses or load film whilst thinking about something else, or even whilst holding a conversation. The camera is now part of you, an extension of your arm and your brain. You have no need to worry that the camera might be set to the wrong film-speed anymore, you have gone through every possible routine, perhaps hundreds of times, until it is as automatic as breathing.

Now to the actual event; we'll continue the wedding theme. You've never photographed a wedding before, so you have no actual experience. You've only been as a guest, or maybe as a participant, so your knowledge of the sequence of events is a little sketchy. Once again, become totally familiar with the order of things and list all possible 'photo opportunities', starting with the most obvious, gradually filling in the gaps. Commit your thoughts and ideas to paper and treat the whole sequence of events as carefully as an army general might plan a battle.

Imagine all that could go wrong (as we did earlier), and then some more. Use your imagination to the extreme, tackling all eventualities; solving each problem one at a time. You've lived it in your mind. You've done a difficult wedding with touchy step-fathers, grouchy grandma's, and spoiled children, all in the pouring rain in January. You never lost control of the situation, you enlisted the help of ushers and/ or the best man to get, and keep, the people where they should be and you have learned to build up groups. You've smiled at everybody (and meant it), even allowing the guests to use their Instamatics over your shoulder; confident in your new professionalism that, now, is quite real. You imagined it all in your mind's eye and won through! You did a difficult wedding and enjoyed it. The bride's mother even thanked you specially!

Because the nervous system can't tell the difference between a real experience and an imagined one, now you actually *are* experienced;

so far as you and your mind are concerned. You visualised it all and you are what you think you are. Professional!

These principles apply to just about any scenario you care to think of, including difficult interviews. Simply be there in your mind, tackling all eventualities as they might arise and soon you'll be an old hand at most things. Before you know it those real-but-imaginary experiences will be reinforced by real-life ones. And who will know the difference? Your nervous system won't! Believe me, there is no difference!

Because you are now totally familiar with all your photographic equipment, you are also free of the shackles of blinding technicalities and free to concentrate on creating pictures. That is what you are paid for. You are certainly not paid to worry!

The foregoing advice comes with a 'public health warning'. This formula works so well there is a real danger you could get complacent. It's possible to become so 'cool' you could almost fall asleep! So, to avoid over-confidence, make each assignment a personal challenge to improve your technique and 'bedside manner' and, above all, be systematic and in control of every situation and, don't forget, have fun!

Invite to a Wedding.

There is a recognised set procedure for carrying out wedding photography, amounting to being in a certain place at a prescribed time, and arranging groups of people and individuals in a time-honoured fashion so you may photograph them. This is an over-simplification of the basis of wedding photography but many people manage with that itinerary alone. They obtain a photographic record of the happy event, trusting in the joyous occasion to give life and colour to their results.

Most of the time the client is happy if the results are sharp and colourful and there is at least one good shot of the bride looking radiant and tolerably lovely, one of the bride and 'groom where he looks handsome and caring and, hopefully, you haven't missed important relatives off the groups! If it takes so little to please the paying customer, surely something must be wrong with the present state of wedding photography!

Let us see what we can do to change our attitude to weddings. After all, much of the event revolves around the photographer who has been elected to capture the occasion on film forever. Not a responsibility to be treated too lightly, but it won't help to be overawed by the fear of failing. You can, and should, come through a wedding on a 'high' equivalent to three glasses of champagne and you will, if you follow a prescribed set of rules. Not only will you actually enjoy the responsibility, but your enthusiasm will be conveyed to all present, ensuring peace of mind to those at the top table, and future big photographic orders from all those present.

As always your approach, attitude and final results will be rewarded, not only financially but in kudos and job-satisfaction. The results you obtain will be 100% better for your enthusiasm and cheerfulness, for this is one occasion where your own infectious happiness will help make the day. Truly, with weddings, you have to be 'more than just a photographer'.

Rules.
Regardless of the size of wedding, it is essential to instil confidence in your client and that usually means the bride's mother or father. They want to feel content that they have hired the right person, so it's up to you to prove your competence and caring, thus confirming their good judgment in choosing you to help make the day. As a wedding photographer, it is expected you will be charming, skilled, and efficient, probably in that order, but above all things you must be genuine and you can't possibly be that if you aren't determined to enjoy your work.

For 'starters', you must involve yourself with all the personalities concerned. This can be done in several ways. Note down names carefully on the first meeting, or telephone contact. Christian names of bride and 'groom, surnames of both families and where the ceremony is to be held. Absorb these details as soon as possible by re-reading them to yourself and writing them down in your diary. It is not a good thing to forget a client's, or a prospective client's, name and, for some, it is the ultimate insult. They can feel offended, and often belittled, to think their own name not worth remembering!

Don't think I am exaggerating. I know from personal experience that a photographer can painlessly graduate from a shot-gun wedding at the local registry office to a fashionable Cathedral wedding with choir, organ, bells, and the full regalia. And you can effect this transformation in the space of a few weeks.

Let's recap, and look at further ways in which we can 'get it right', and accumulate goodwill and experience.

It is desirable that, after you have made the booking in your diary, you arrange to meet the bride's family and, if this is the first contact you have had with them, you dress suitably. There is no need for a suit and dickie-bow, but you must be clean and well turned-out to create the right impression from the start. Appear cheerful without being raucous or silly, and wait for positive signs before making too many assumptions about the family. Let them set the scene at this juncture, because you probably know nothing of their ways. You're not a funeral director, but it's as well to tread carefully in case there are any sensitive elements to be considered. For instance, when discussing the ceremony you wouldn't say, "Will granny be there?" She might just have died and you would be responsible for reminding them. Show some diplomacy and be sensitive to their feelings and privacy, if that is what is called for.

Chances are they will all be in good spirits and looking forward to the big day. It is a very big occasion for them, with lots of arrangements to make to ensure everything runs like clockwork. Engaging your services is just a part of it, and they need to feel reassured that they can leave the photography in your capable hands. Go through the planned proceedings with them, mentioning all the normal photo-opportunities, finding out the name of the officiating minister and his attitude to photography in the church.

This should be straightforward enough, but remember to make notes of everything. Never simply commit it to memory, it can't be done, even with a family you know well! Assuming they are confident in your ability, you then need to discuss the question of fees. It is quite normal to accept a deposit payment at this stage to secure the appointment in your diary. Having successfully concluded that part of things, your next task is to visit the church, or registry office, to familiarise yourself with the scene of action, taking in all the possible areas offering good backgrounds. Note the aspect of the church doorway in relation to the sun, but, if it is not out, you may need to use your compass (that you always carry!). This might be a good opportunity to see the officiating clergyman, so make some preliminary enquiries, bearing in mind you can always return to finalise your plans for a trouble-free wedding.

There is usually quite a span of time between booking a wedding photographer and the actual ceremony, so you will have plenty of time to organise everything that concerns you. You will need to check over *all* your equipment and make sure you have a good supply of film you are totally familiar with. There must be no areas of doubt on the forthcoming day, so take no chances if you wish to enjoy your 'wedding'.

In the meantime, unless you already know what you are going to do, it would be of great advantage to do some homework in readiness. Everybody has some idea of wedding photography but you need to be the master here, so swallow your pride and do some study. This unashamedly means looking at wedding pictures taken by established professionals, both in shop windows and in books on the subject. There is no disgrace in it, regard it as 'research' if you like. You are simply sifting through other people's work to build up your own repertoire. This doesn't mean you cannot be original, but there is no law against copying either. Imitation is the sincerest form of flattery after all. Even if you tried to copy exactly a particular pose, it would never be *quite* the same because the 'models' are different and so is the scenery.

Let's face it. 'Bride of the Year' can only be successful if the people and background are reasonably attractive to start with, plus some decent weather of course. Naturally, even with all the best ingredients, you still have to pose your subjects to some degree. The success of this is usually a case of creating a relaxed atmosphere on the day.

On the wedding day, arrive at the church in good time so that you are relaxed from the very start. You certainly have to be there before anything happens so as to catch the 'groom with his 'best man'. You might even have had to call at the brides house before that, to photograph the fun and games there though, from my experience, it is often bedlam and pandemonium.

The photographer is usually a key figure at any wedding and he has a lot of influence over the whole mood of the event. It's an opportunity to build up a style and 'bedside manner' that will hold you in good stead forever. You can be entertaining and funny, or even dress differently to everybody else if you wish, in order to do your job efficiently and reasonably quickly. It doesn't hurt to stand out in the crowd. That way you can command everybody's attention when you need to! If the weather is beautiful and warm, and everybody is showing off their finery, it could be that the whole assembly would *prefer* you to extend the photography bit. This event has cost a small fortune, some are wearing clothes they don't ever expect to wear again, so it stands to reason they won't want to hasten the proceedings unless it's freezing cold or pouring down with rain! When the wedding details were planned, a certain length of time was allotted for photographs, so why cheat the family by being in an unseemly rush?

In a way, your presence glamourises the occasion (in the true sense of the word) and your role of recording the event in full glorious technicolour is an important one. I have seldom found anything but respect and helpfulness toward the photographer. After all, if guests misbehave in any way, you have your camera at the ready to capture the episode.

Find out who the key figures are, if you don't already have this information, and you might be able to recruit them to assist at times. It could be a revered uncle, or a maiden aunt with a loud voice, but more likely an usher or an active father-figure. Either way he, or she, can help you 'round up' guests when you are building groups – starting with the bride and 'groom, then adding bridesmaids, page-boys and parents. When you still have the 'stars' of the show before your camera, you can bring in immediate relatives from both families, then aunts, uncles and grand-parents, if present. But definitely do not call for the bride's grandfather – unless you know him to be alive and well!

Find out these things beforehand, diplomatically! There are various permutations when grouping after this, usually constituting bringing in special friends, distant relatives and guests, not necessarily in that order. Always ask the bride and 'groom if they would like any 'special' photographs taken. (No, I don't mean *that* sort of picture!) The bride may particularly like a photograph of herself with her friends from work, or with a specially dear relative who has travelled all the way from Australia to be with her on her special day.

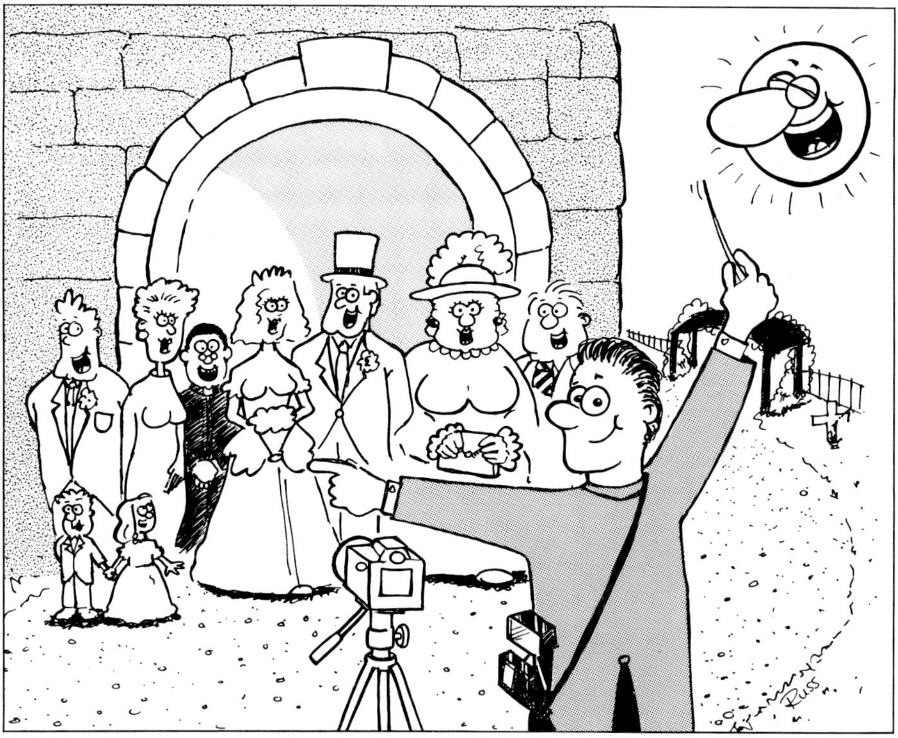

Enquiring is always appreciated, and your special concern is always noted.

Throughout all the foregoing proceedings, you will have acted professionally and calmly, with supreme confidence and authority. You will have been considerate to other camera-users, managed to control the crowd (as much as is ever possible) and, throughout all this, taken lots of pictures using all your ingenuity, and some of other people's as well. It will be an enjoyable experience, for you and all present. Now take the usual 'confetti and Rolls Royce' pictures (giving your own variations on a theme), then back to the reception or 'wedding breakfast', where you will be thanked profusely for your trouble!

But it is no trouble! In honesty you will have enjoyed every minute and it only took an hour or so! You will be invited to stay for the meal and, of course, take pictures – and you get to kiss the bride too! What a lovely life it is – and you are being paid as well!

It's strange how the good word travels and, as in all aspects of business, personal recommendation is the best form of advertising. It is also reassuring, satisfying and a good deal cheaper than any other form of self-promotion. When your name is put forward because of your past successes, you *know* you are getting it right!

CHAPTER TWELVE.

Sun, Wind and Weather.

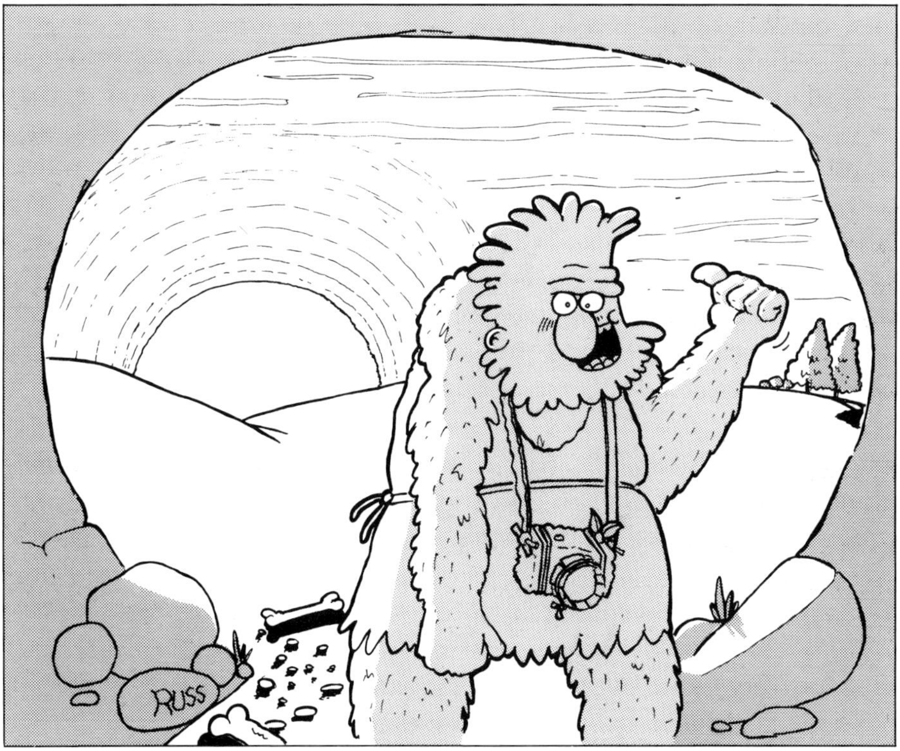

'THAT BIG RED THING HAS JUST COME UP AGAIN!'

It is no wonder that past civilisations worshipped the sun. Many thousands of years ago, at the dawn of man's evolution, it was realised that the big red thing that came up over the horizon every morning was the giver of life. And still today our very existence depends totally upon that same sun rising. It gives us heat and light, and thus our plantlife and food. Not just for us, but also the animals that sustain us. We know that if the sun went out, life on earth would cease and everything living would quickly die. But we still take this miracle for granted. Even as photographers we expect the sun to appear at regular intervals; and it does. I do think photographers are less likely to take the sun for granted than most, we are more aware of its passage through the heavens because of what we do. Perhaps even more aware than farmers who seem to complain constantly about the weather, and maybe as much as thinking architects who ought to take into account the sun's seasonal trajectories in order to make the most of its natural (and free) light and heat.

In the studio, when we are re-creating a controlled condition to imitate natural light, we tend to have one main light source, either direct or diffused and fill-in the resultant shadows as perhaps clouds might. That is the joy of studio lighting. Controlling everything to simulate a natural condition, regardless of the weather outside. Here, on Earth, we have one sun and, consequently, use one main modelling light. If we lived on a planet with two suns, we would think that having two shadows was quite normal and no doubt re-create that condition instead, then all those marvellous film star portraits by 'Karsh of Ottowa' would look quite wrong.

There's food for thought. But, though the sun, and whether it shines or not, is a major factor in our line of business, we seem to be more concerned with the actual weather. And most of the British are.

The study of our weather is a huge subject but we must, as photographers, take a more than passing interest in those natural forces that control all our lives to such a great extent. For a nation, whose national pastime seems to be talking about the weather, we generally know very little about the subject. Indeed, most people only care whether it is going to be cold or hot, windy or calm, wet or dry. Without doubt the changeable British weather is a daily topic of conversation for most people on these Isles, where television weather forecasters have celebrity status!

Of course we don't want to get soaked when we have forgotten the umbrella, or find ourselves snowbound miles from home. Sadly, cricket matches are rained-off, weddings ruined and holidays washed out but, as photographers, our very livelihoods are actually threatened by the vagaries of our British climate.

Certainly we need to know more than most about what lies ahead; for today, tomorrow, or even next week, so that we can, with reasonable confidence, organise our diaries and cope with what the weather has in store.

We cannot control the weather, but merely plan around those difficult spells and make the most of the better ones; and in times of doubt when deadlines are pressing, we have to take calculated risks, supported perhaps by up-to-date forecasts, intuition, optimism, or maybe a lump of seaweed.

When a job has been fixed ahead, and it is important that you have the correct weather conditions, you will no doubt have discussed the forthcoming weather with your client. Perhaps by telephone, either the day or evening before the event or, better still, first thing in the morning of the day in question. Almost without exception, the client takes his cue from the photographer, believing he is the expert on such matters and that we have a hot-line to God! It is assumed, and expected, that you will predict what the weather is going to do during the whole day so that he, the client, does not have to worry on that score. He can concentrate solely on his side of the organising. He leaves the weather to you. If it is pouring with rain when you speak to your client, and you say that in half an hour you will both be basking in glorious sunshine, the chances are he will believe you. He trusts you to know these things and, in a way, you can – you certainly must try. So how is it possible?

The Meteorology Department in this country is still funded by the Government. It is considered important enough to be run by the Ministry of Defence and countless millions are spent annually in an effort to accurately predict the weather so that national catastrophe does not catch us out. Despite expensive computer-aided forecasting, we all know that the final forecast is down to a team of educated people who must interpret all the information fed from space satellites and Earth-bound weather stations, not just in the U.K., but on a much larger international scale encompassing the whole of the northern hemisphere at least. We also know that, despite all this technology, the weatherman can still get it wrong. And, when huge areas of woodland are flattened by "freak" storms in the middle of the night bringing the country into a state of emergency, we ask ourselves "Why?"

The plain fact is that in our temperate zone, surprises are always just around the corner. Headlines like "Wettest June for Forty Years", "Coldest August for Twenty Years", "Mildest December for Fifteen Years", and so on, drive home the lesson that we should never be complacent about the weather. There is no simple pattern of events, such as you might find in countries where the prevailing weather conditions are stabilised by the country's size or geographical position. Our relatively tiny island sits between the huge continental land mass of Europe and the very wet Atlantic Ocean, where most of our prevailing winds come from. Even though we are subjected to many conflicting air currents from all directions, Nature abhors a vacuum, and is always trying to equalise its forces of swirling air currents, all of varying strength, temperature, humidity and barometric pressure. Computers can cope very well with this information but we have to remember that the 'picture' is not a two dimensional one, but has depth as well. And those higher jet streams many miles up are making their influence felt. Therein lies the biggest problem, and the reason for many inaccurate forecasts.

So how can all of this help us? Firstly, because we must have some faith in professional advice of any description, we must pay attention to what the weatherman has to say. Although his predictions are frequently supported by cartoon-like diagrams, covering very general areas of country that never seem to apply to the area we are specifically interested in, more revealing to me are the quick flashes of actual satellite photographs assembled into a short time-lapse film. These are actual photographs and when I see these I can appreciate the whole scenario and form my own conclusions about cloud density, wind direction and strength, relating to that part of the country where I shall be operating. I am not too interested in cartoon pictures of clouds with cartoon-rain falling from them. The general public, for whom these pretty (but rather vague), pictures seem to be drawn, are really not so concerned about accuracy as photographers might be. Most people only need to decide whether to do the washing, if its worth washing the car or watering the garden.

Forecast-wise, farmers have a slightly better deal and fairly accurate long-range forecasts are screened once a week. Find out precisely when this is (at weekends) and catch it if you can.

Now that the telephone industry has been privatised, you can't ring the weather forecast as you used to – cheaply. Instead there is a more comprehensive one-day or long-range forecast (depending how long you hang on) which covers specific and smaller areas of the country. These telephone calls are very expensive and could cost more than two pounds a time, depending on whether you heard all of the recorded message first time around.

Possibly the most accurate, and certainly up-to-the-minute, information is obtained from Air Traffic Control centres all over the country. Lives can be at stake where flying is concerned and every effort is made to keep these centres of information precise and totally current. Unfortunately, such information is not readily available to the general public, unless you personally subscribe to the service.

When you are seriously considering chartering an aeroplane or helicopter to undertake aerial photography you are in a position to request such information through the charter company, who usually have an annual subscription to this enhanced weather service. I use this service, but it is always supported by other sources of information.

'VOLMET', so far unmentioned, is one of these. This is not a forecast in the true sense of the word, more an up-to-date state of affairs covering all the major air-traffic areas. It is in existence to assist pilots traversing the country. I'm sure very few readers will even have heard of it, because it is transmitted on a 'strange' frequency. If you wish to know what the weather is doing in Bristol you could, of course, ring a friend or client in that area and ask him to look out of the window to see what is happening there, but non-professional individuals are never accurate. You are only likely to learn if the sun is shining or if it is raining. You won't get the whole picture, only his opinion. If you ask him how much cloud cover there is, he will probably say "Not a lot", whereas VOLMET would tell you "three octas (three eighths cloud) at 5,000 feet, and one octa at 20,000 feet". That is accurate enough to know you will have some sunshine through the gaps, so long as that condition continues. VOLMET will also give you temperature, wind speed, visibility, barometric pressure, etc which, once you have mastered the jargon, should prove useful. VOLMET SOUTH covers the south of England up to Birmingham Airport, VOLMET NORTH, on a different frequency, covers northern England and all of Scotland. This information is regularly updated at twenty minute intervals. Unfortunately, you cannot telephone VOLMET, it is transmitted non-stop on an aircraft frequency and you need the proper equipment to receive it. This can take the form of a VHF radio with extended reception capable of receiving air traffic conversations, or by the use of a frequency scanner. With this latter piece of equipment you merely enter the frequencies you wish to monitor and it scans them all in seconds; or you can stop at any frequency manually to listen in to that one only.

You cannot transmit on these aircraft frequencies unless you are a fully-fledged radio operator who has passed the necessary exams. But that is not our concern here, our goal is to gain as much information as we can, to enable us to perform our photographic duties to the best of our ability.

Other, much simpler, forecasting methods are readily available to us all. Photographers, perhaps because of their calling, tend to be observant individuals. If they are not so to begin with they become that way with time. Photographers spend much more time than most looking up at the skies. Like a shepherd or fisherman whose livelihood, comfort and safety depend upon reading the weather, we too become reasonably proficient at such things by applying the adage 'necessity is the mother of invention'. I occasionally amaze people by saying "Get your washing in, it will be raining in five minutes time!" No magic involved! Falling rain can be seen a mile or two away and, if the wind is blowing in your direction, it stands to reason it will arrive pretty soon. How soon depends upon the wind speed. Also certain cloud formations are rain-bearing, giving showery conditions with sunny spells in between. Cloud formations can also tell us quite a lot about what to expect ahead and there are books available to guide us in this art.

I don't pretend to fully understand barometric pressures, but I do know that when the isobars are close together on weather maps we can expect windy conditions. The 'deeper' the 'low', the greater the wind, and in the 'eye' of a low or high we can expect calmer conditions. But, in a way, I prefer windy conditions to most others. We tend not to get wind in this country without broken cloud of some sort and featureless skies are quite characterless unless we strongly filter them. Those long spells of hot weather that we have experienced in recent Summers are invariably hazy days of rather insipid skies, making it necessary to filter quite heavily. Whereas unsettled showery spells frequently bring clearer conditions, with sometimes dramatic cloud formations that make a photographers life a happier one. At least when it's windy the clouds are moving quickly and, should we need sunshine, then we won't have long to wait. Also, with some cloud about, the colour temperature of the light is nearer to that to which films are manufactured, whereas clear blue skies give harsh empty blue shadows, not having the advantage of clouds to fill-in the shadows.

Hot hazy days can sometimes be saved by the use of graduated filters, polarisers, or combinations of two or more filters. The haze may be airborne dust or moisture with no filterable tone of blue near the horizon and, in extreme cases, no blue at the zenith either. In these conditions, colour temperature is close to the 5600 degrees Kelvin norm.

When those graduated filters first became available, not so many years ago, it was the amateur photographer who first took them seriously. Perhaps my own disinterested attitude was indicative of professionals at the time. I must admit I was sceptical about using them because I had fears of losing both quality and realism in my photographs. Probably because I had seen some pretty awful examples of multi-coloured skies with no soft transition. They were simply over-the-top and quite unnatural-looking. However, with patience and trial and error, I 'cracked it' as they say. It was all about choosing the correct F-stop to focal-length combination to get the necessary control. When using wide angle or ultra-wide angle lenses with their enormous depth of field characteristics, don't be frightened to hold the filter right up close to the front lens element, not using the screw-on filter-holder at all. These days I must admit that I don't travel far without a good selection of such filters. They have often saved a picture from being rather dull or uninteresting and when I discovered that clients liked the results, I was hooked. As with all things, the keyword is moderation.

Heavens Above.

This may sound condescending but ask anybody where the sun rises and they will say, "In the East, even a child knows that", and they might add that it sets in the West for good measure! So it does, more or less, but "more or less" is not accurate enough for any thinking photographer. Ask the same person which direction is East and he is not so sure; his knowledge seems to end there.

Two or three thousand years ago the ancient Greeks, Romans and even the Brits for that matter were far more familiar with the skies than we are today. Perhaps this is the result of there being less to amuse people in those days but, more likely because it mattered more to them. Even fifty years ago, millions of country folk got up when it became light and went to bed when darkness fell. Their lives revolved around the Seasons, the sun and the elements.

Photographers today can say the same to some extent, we are not brought up to it from the cradle, so to speak; we find out by observation because we need to know. It's very helpful to know that the sun actually shines upon a North-facing building in mid-Summer, when the daylight-hours last from three-thirty in the morning until after ten o'clock at night. That's more than eighteen hours! By comparison, in December days are no more than eight hours long, or should we say short! That is really important! So, in mid-Summer the sun must rise somewhere in the North-East and set in the North-West and the height it reaches in the sky in June can be as much as eighty degrees above the horizon. In Winter, at midday, the sun can barely manage fifteen degrees above the horizon and the usable portion of the daylight hours is limited to about four hours in the middle of the day, unless you are photographing a sunrise or sunset.

If, in December, the sun doesn't manage to climb more than fifteen degrees up from the horizon then, apart from shorter daylight hours, it naturally means much longer shadows. In these circumstances, even at midday, a ten-foot high wall will throw a shadow that is practically forty foot long. Certainly not good for aerial photography in towns, but ideal in open countryside to reveal undulations in the terrain, unnoticed in Summer at the same time of day. I guess the lesson is, when conditions seem against you, sometimes it is possible to make them work for you.

Do please note that if you consider the path of the sun around the Earth as a complete circle of three-hundred and sixty degrees then, in Winter, it only makes an appearance for ninety degrees of it. Not really enough, but we are stuck with it, I'm afraid.

Because I believe it matters enough, I have actually taken compass bearings of the sun at noted times of the day and plotted its course on paper using a circular protractor. I found that the sun moves approximately fifteen degrees an hour, depending on its trajectory through the skies. You might think I've flipped my lid, but this sort of information is quite invaluable when trying to calculate the optimum time for photographing a specific building, or doing aerial photography of a site you have never visited. No doubt my friends think me a little weird but, for some reason, my clients have gained the impression that I care about what I do. Certainly I take my work seriously, and I enjoy it. Making up to a thousand pounds per day should be taken seriously!

It is said, as a photographer, you should not travel without a camera. Also on my list of less-obvious photographic paraphernalia I include two magnetic compasses, one is fixed in the car for navigation and observation, the other is of the hand-held type with graduations in degrees relative to magnetic North. Sometimes, to obtain the best possible results, I often have to make return visits, when the light is in the best position, to achieve an effect I want. With a compass, and armed with my chart, I can calculate this optimum time, even back at the studio if I wish. Maybe this 'making charts' seems a lot of trouble, but you only have to do it once. The act of 'doing' seems to imprint it into your memory banks. Anything you do to take the guesswork out of your photography has to give you an edge over the competition.

This may also appear to be taking things too far but I also have two clocks in my studio. One set for Greenwich Mean Time and the other labelled British Summer Time. This way, I can never forget which way the time should be adjusted; because if you guess wrongly you could be two hours in error, not just one.

Moon observations (unless you happen to be a werewolf!) are of lesser importance to most of us but a few pointers are worth mentioning. Whereas the rising and setting of the sun only varies by a minute or so each day, that is not the case with the moon. The daily difference of moon-rise is practically an hour but, without referring to your diary or to your daily newspaper, it is difficult to calculate because you quickly lose track unless you note it every day. Even I don't go that far! We also know that full-moon occurs once each lunar month, approximately every twenty-eight days. It is worth noting that full-moon rise does happen to coincide with the setting of the sun once each lunar month and, on these occasions when I have been photographing a sunset, it is monthly possible to turn around and focus your attentions and camera, on the moon.

Not many people have tried, successfully, to photograph the moon because, to do it properly, a very long lens is needed. In fact, to fill a 35mm frame you require something like a 2000mm focal length lens, and even then there are special problems. It goes without saying that, with such a long lens, you need an exceptionally sturdy tripod. I use two, one fore and one aft, for maximum stability. But, having solved that problem, you will soon find, if you watch through the viewfinder, the moon literally races across the screen. (We know it is not the moon moving, but the Earth rotating, that gives this impression). To combat the image movement, I find you have to give at least one-fifteenth of a second exposure and, if you are using delayed action to trigger your shutter, you literally have to predict where the moon will be in your viewfinder at the time of exposure. Otherwise, you will only get a 'half-moon'.

On the question of exposure, unless you have the luxury of a spot-meter with an acceptance angle of about one degree, you will have to use test-runs to get it right. I like to photograph the full-moon just after the sun has set because, as the sun sinks down on the western horizon, the moon rises on the diagonally opposite side where the sky tends to slowly turn from pale blue to a lovely shade of deep blue-purple. This makes a perfect background, not just for moon shots, but for any number of subjects. If you want to photograph the moon's craters, you will find, when the moon is full, you have the least amount of modelling on the full-frontally lit moon; so it appears rather flat. Pictorially it might be better to get it before half-moon when it is crescent-shaped. A good exposure starting point, with 100 ASA film, could be one fifteenth at F8 to F11 depending on the atmosphere. Recently, on a very clear night out in the country, I recorded an exposure of one-thirtieth at F16. The moon was so bright that, with the naked eye, it appeared burnt-out, requiring dark-glasses to look at it! So please expect the unexpected.

I did suggest, near the beginning of this chapter, that this was a large and seemingly endless subject and, to cover it comprehensively, could be a book in itself. But, before I leave it, there is one important area that I must cover briefly in order to give you the best possible advantage over the uninitiated! It concerns using our unusual weather to our own ends.

So often of late, whilst I have been struggling to achieve out of the ordinary pictures, I have been conscious of certain freak conditions that happen from time to time. Try using these conditions, like dramatic storm-clouds instead of fluffy white clouds, as a backdrop. Or maybe the filtered murk of smoke from burning stubble in the fields to contrast white buildings, or wait for rays of sunshine to strike the right part of a picture. There are many examples, and luck and patience are involved; but each time, for me, it has resulted in the capturing of photographs hitherto out of the reach of my imagination. I suppose this could come under the heading of 'breaking new ground', even though it is not a new idea. Usually, when rain-stops-play, photographers pack up and go home. Next time don't! Simply put your equipment in the car and stay at the ready. Give nature the benefit of the doubt, and be patient. It could make your day! My own stock library has gained some nice new additions this way. When something new or different is created, and it meets with approval from the paying client, then not only does it make me happy, it gives me a renewed sense of purpose – and that's what drives me on!

So keep a weather eye open for opportunities, you can't control the weather or the heavens but you can make sure you're there when everything is working for you. If you can't make friends with the elements, at least learn to understand them, because it's the only way you can win. Then, with patience and the will to achieve, you can boost your output enormously, just by caring enough to succeed ...despite, or because of, the weather.

Survival.

Some might say 'survival' sounds a little melodramatic! After all, we are talking mainly about photography in the U.K, not on the north face of the Eiger or in Death Valley USA! So where's the problem? Well, take it from me, there are all sorts of reasons why we have to know about survival and self-preservation in the pursuit of our chosen profession – to do it properly, that is. Sure, you can tie yourself to the studio, where your only problem might be running out of milk and sugar, but you will still be potentially at risk, particularly if you are handling studio lighting. So it goes without saying that you certainly need to know how to change a fuse, at least.

As with all risks we can do certain things to reduce the odds so that those risks are insignificant.

Our objective is to carry on our work safely, in reasonable comfort wherever possible, and to the best of our ability. This can't be achieved without looking ahead at potential hazards. There is no way we can function efficiently if we are frozen to the marrow, soaking wet or dehydrated with by the heat of the day, and I would definitely add "starving" to that list. My own metabolism requires that I eat regularly and, although I've never fainted with hunger yet, it has been close at times. Always try to ensure that you have a snack of some kind close at hand. It can be almost a life-saver when you're out in the wilds, miles from home. Even a packet of biscuits can make all the difference.

More understandably we should include 'extreme cold' in our look at survival. Every winter I take on jobs which entail standing out in very cold conditions and this is probably our most common cause for concern. It's often not until we've been out of our heated car for ten minutes or so that we start to wish that we had worn something more suitable. Because we live in a temperate zone, we tend to think that we will never encounter real cold, not like you might experience in Siberia, for instance. Try telling that to anyone who has stood on a hillside in a high wind during January. If you are improperly dressed you could be unconscious in a couple of hours and, if nobody knows you are there, you could die. The wind, together with even minus one or two degrees, can have a extremely chilling effect, making it feel like minus ten. All natural body heat is taken away with the wind and even a few minutes of this can make you quickly understand how old people die from hypothermia. You have to experience something like this to even halfway know what it feels like.

You will soon be aware of feeling intensely cold, unable to create body heat quicker than it is being robbed from your shivering frame. This is speedily followed by involuntary shaking, light-headedness, and pain – all this in England too. You pick up your tripod and it feels like your hands are stuck to the cold metal. The tears are streaming down your face and you wonder if you are crying with the cold and the agony, or from the wind that has proved to you that the elements cannot be beaten, unless you are well prepared. In practice, of course, except for the exceptionally stubborn, a hasty retreat will be beaten to the car long before the pain sets in, telling yourself that you've photographed all you can in the circumstances, proving that discretion is the better part of valour.

So what should you have done? Well, because you are used to checking your equipment requirements before each assignment, it's highly unlikely you will have forgotten any of your camera gear. But you simply weren't properly equipped!

One layer of clothing wasn't enough, and you now know you can lose an enormous amount of body heat through the top of your head by not wearing a suitable hat. OK! So you don't wear hats! But there have to be exceptions, so forget your street-cred and find either a cap or woolly hat, a balaclava helmet or anorak-hood etc.

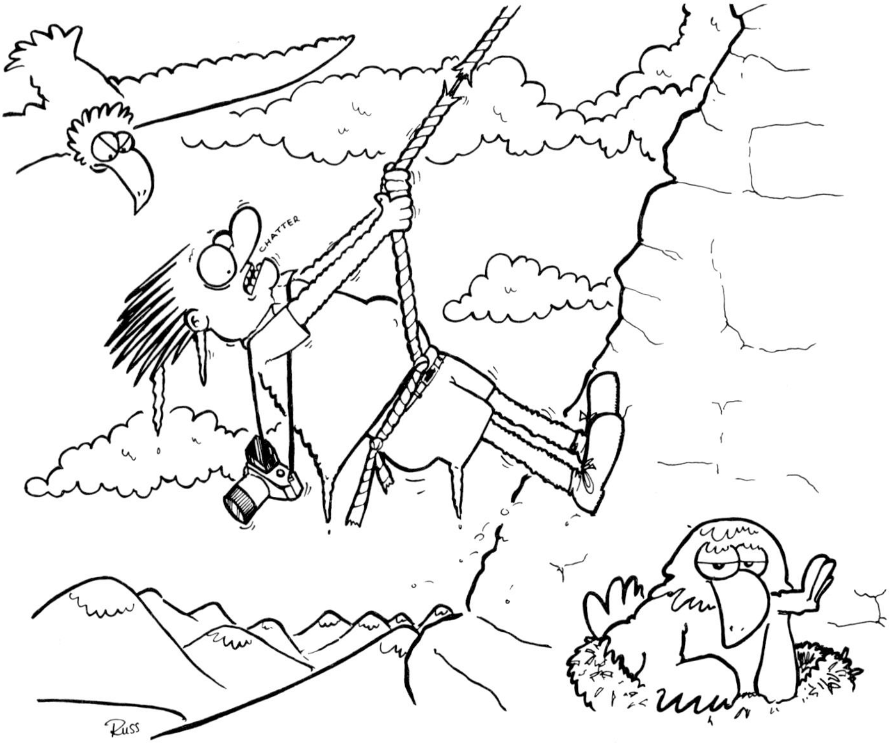

I'm sure I felt you cringe at the mention of "anorak" just then. If that's not good for your image, find an alternative more your scene. Anything is better than frostbite! What **is** important is, unless you cover your head, you could fail to get your pictures!

It was such a day on Exmoor a few years ago when I decided enough was enough and I wanted to live, so I retreated to the pretty harbour of Lynmouth to thaw-out in a large run-down-but-warm hotel. After getting the feeling back in my extremities, I had time to ponder the situation and ventured out again. This time to the shops for a sheep-skin coat!

I had earned it, I deserved it, and I've never regretted it!

NOTES

CHAPTER THIRTEEN.

Aerial Photography.

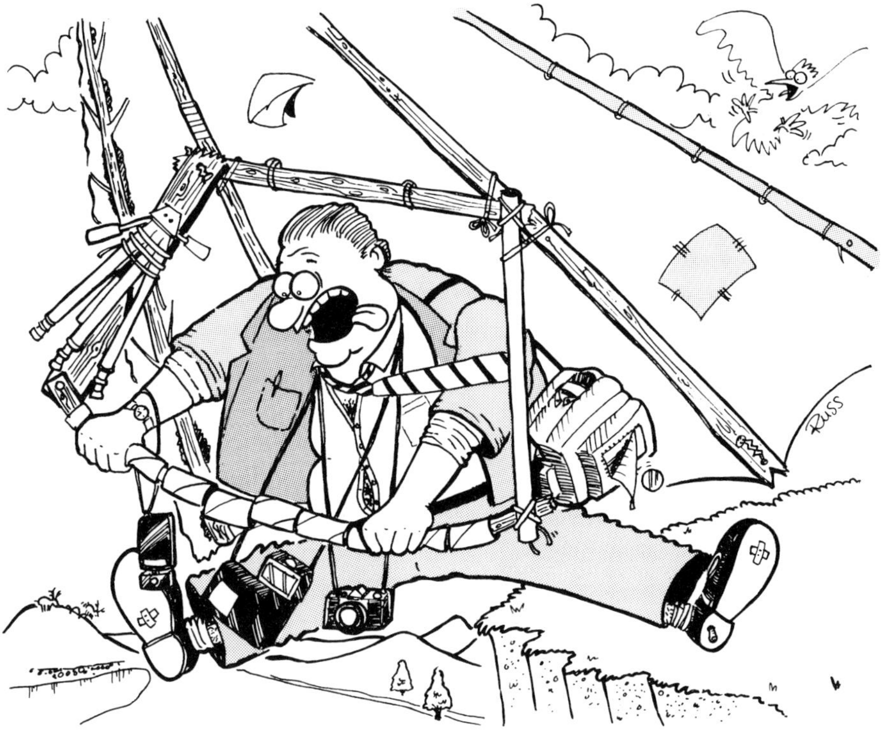

Going up in the World.

Most people are afraid of aerial photography. Not necessarily of falling out of the sky, but of the high costs of flying in relation to their potential success rate. Having tried it once, and failed or been disappointed, they are reluctant to risk it again. You can put this down to inexperience, an inability to adapt to a different environment or, more usually, approaching it with the wrong attitude. You must expect teething troubles, when embarking on some new sphere of photography. The purpose of this chapter is to pass on some experience so that, having lived it in your mind, it becomes an experience of your very own.

Although it stands to reason that certain people could feel apprehensive about flying, and of putting their lives in the hands of another individual (namely the pilot), such phobias can easily be put into perspective, especially when weighing any possible risks against the rewards of achievement, both financial and of a more personal nature. Being an accomplished aerial photographer makes a professional photographer a genuine all-rounder, instilling real confidence in himself and in his clients.

Looking first at the fear of failing, the same principles applied when taking wedding photographs apply here. If you are confident of your ability to produce the goods, and have faith in your equipment, you are three parts there. The rest is down to learning a few tricks and having the right attitude. If you can take picture on the ground, why should it be any harder from a mobile platform in the sky?

Aerial photographs can be taken on almost any modern-day camera. Whereas I prefer medium format, there is an acclaimed expert in the USA who never uses anything but Nikon; his results are excellent because he has tailored his technique to suit. The only real criteria I can see are those concerning the viewfinder, which should be either pentaprism or wire-frame, using a lens that performs adequately at infinity, and having a total familiarity with your choice of camera. Always flying with a back-up camera body is desirable, although I have never needed to resort to my second Mamiya. A choice of filters is definitely an insurance against the dreaded haze problem; and a good exposure metering system is a necessity.

That only leaves you, the aircraft, and the weather. In other words, chartering the aircraft when conditions are right, both from a weather point of view and choosing the right time of day, or even year. For instance, the very clear conditions that precede forthcoming rain are absolutely ideal. On a good day it is possible to see more than fifty miles from this elevated 'platform' but, if you can see no further than five to ten miles, then you are probably wasting your time, unless you are operating at very low-level. There aren't many days that are perfect, so we usually have to settle for less. Our biggest weather problem is that of visibility, and when it is 'poor' no amount of filtering will rectify the situation. This is usually decided before actually taking off, and is an acquired skill.

Haze shows up worst, and is exaggerated, when you are looking into the light; so looking south-east at the morning horizon will tell you a lot. That bluish atmosphere may be dust, moisture, smoke or a combination of all three. When it's severe it can't be overcome, so we simply have no choice but to wait for it to clear, which may happen if the wind picks up. Being aware of our natural environment is very much part of being a professional photographer so, when driving around the countryside, start taking a real interest in the weather that surrounds you, especially when you are on high ground, and before you know it you will have become an expert weather-reader. (You can read more of this in the chapter on "Sun, Wind and Weather").

Now to consider the fear of falling. Again, this is in your own hands to a large extent. You might employ a 'cowboy' outfit to courier some prints cross-country, but you would be silly to put your faith, and your life, in the hands of some reckless, inexperienced pilot who has an aeroplane that resembles an untidy crows nest (held together with shit and sticks). There are enough charter companies in existence to be spoiled for choice, particularly with helicopters, because they are a growth industry. My own files contain at least six local companies who hire-out helicopters by the day, the hour, or even half-hour. Their rates are not cheap, because helicopters are not cheap to buy, or to insure. Neither are they cheap to service and their servicing schedules come round every fifty hours, as laid down by the Civil Aviation Authority, for everyone's safety. Also pilots, like photographers, are paid quite handsomely, so you can easily be talking about £400 per hour to hire a helicopter. This doesn't mean to say that you can't do a deal with the hire company, I always do, it would be silly not to. The more you fly, the better the rates you can negotiate. Whether you pay 'full whack' or not, you can pass on the full cost of the charter flight to your own client, on a separate invoice if you wish, and keep your bill for operating time and materials etc. as a separate issue. Your own time should be charged at a higher rate than for ground work, taking into account such things as the extra expertise needed (not a lot!), the dead-time spent organising and planning the flight, waiting for take-off, refuelling, or maybe postponing if the weather has been unsuitable. Even an hour's flying can easily take a half-day of your time.

Your choice of charter company will be affected by the type of aircraft used and, most important in my opinion, the rapport you strike up with the pilot. Let's face it, if you have the necessary equipment and the expertise, plus the helicopter and perfect weather conditions, all this will be wasted if you are saddled with an inexperienced pilot who can't follow your instructions, or has difficulty placing an aircraft at the correct point in the sky. This has happened to me. I even had one 'pilot' who got so lost that I took over the navigation. It's therefore not a bad idea to always have a reasonable notion of where you are, it also makes the trip that much more interesting, and it's not too difficult.

You can't tell, just by looking at a pilot, whether he is a good choice or not. He might have a perfectly white shirt, immaculate epaulettes and fully look the part, but he may be more suited to running air-taxis from A to B than working closely with photographers. Make no mistake, you can't get the best results if you and the pilot are not on the same wavelength. You have to work together. The 'working together' starts in the operations room, where you discuss the job before the flight.

He needs to know precisely where you want to go so, on an ordinance survey map, you point out the target areas. He then decides whether there are any serious obstacles, such as operating within the control-zone of a busy airport, or flying low in a built-up area. It's easy to imagine, especially when you are pounding your car steering-wheel in a traffic-jam on the M25, that the skies are marvelously clear. They can be in some areas, but there are many rules pertaining to flying procedure and air-space. These rules are made with safety in mind, so we should try to understand them. The pilot is the person who would lose his licence to fly should he seriously infringe those rules, so try to understand his point of view, and he will try to understand yours. If you request that he drops down to 200 feet over a built-up area he will say "No way!" If, however, you have permission to land, or hover low over a piece of waste ground or pasture land, then it is a different story.

Try to think of it this way; if you are causing a noise-nuisance by disturbing residents, then it is likely to be illegal. If, by flying too low, you have no escape route in the event of engine failure and are likely to fall on people below, that too is illegal. It may not be comforting to you to realise that the authorities are more concerned for the innocent people you might fall on and not your own safety. But this raises a good point. A 35mm camera falling out of a helicopter window would kill even Arnie Schwarzenegger, should it fall on him at 150 mph.

Back to the ops room, where you are discussing your target site – a factory. If, close to the factory or within its perimeter, there is a suitable landing spot you know is clear of overhead wires and other obstacles, then you can, theoretically, land if you have permission. You may have permission to land but don't actually want to do so, simply using the 'landing' site as a means of coming down to 100 feet or lower. When you don't have permission the only way you can come low over a city is to do a steady low pass on your way to another area for which you do have permission. But all this is entirely subject to the pilot's agreement, and I say it 'off the record'. This kind of planning has to be sorted out well in advance, and the time involved should be noted, and included in your invoice or quote.

So, assuming you have now acquainted your pilot with your sites, and he has cleared all possible problems that you might meet, you are now in business. The aircraft is fuelled up whilst he opens his 'log' and together you walk to the holding area.

You will, of course, be quite prepared equipment-wise and, if the pilot thinks it is necessary, you could be asked to wear warm clothing. Even on a hot summer's day it can be cold at 2000 feet, especially if you have a window open, or the door removed, for better visibility. (Never, ever, shoot through perspex).

War-time pilots didn't wear those sheepskin jackets just for pose-value! You won't be flying Concorde, with air-conditioning and air-hostesses bringing round cocktails. This is more like 'Sopwith Camel and Biggles' stuff, where you feel the wind in your hair.

Next, the pilot does his external pre-flight examination of the control surfaces, and checks for birds' nests in the jet intake. Satisfied that all is well, he ensures you are tucked in safely and that you are familiar with the safety harnesses and intercom system. The headset link with the pilot is very necessary, but it also serves to protect your eardrums from the engine noise (a two or three hour trip without it can leave you temporarily deaf).

The pilot 'rotates' his blades, picking up revs as he does instrument checks, until he's happy that everything is working satisfactorily. Once the engine has warmed up sufficiently, he requests permission from the Air Traffic Controller (ATC) to leave the ground. He can't leave until told to do so, obeying flight procedures to the letter. Even then he must inform ATC how many 'souls' are on board, the purpose of the mission, and where you plan to go. Cleared to leave, it's "Chocks Away!", and the fun begins.

I have to say this. No matter how often one flies, there is always something special about taking-off in a helicopter. Even with a 'boring' pilot, it is interesting; but with an experienced ex-services pilot it can be unforgettable. The aircraft lifts off a few feet, hangs there a second or two, the tail comes up and the nose dips and, as the pilot pours on the power, you are propelled forward, literally held in your seat by the acceleration. The grass and hedges hurtle beneath you as you gain speed and height, cows and trees grow smaller as you rise. No matter how many times you have done this, the novelty doesn't wear off. The view is dramatic, panoramic and constantly changing. There is usually a seat (or two) spare, particularly in a Jet Ranger, and I often take somebody along just for the experience. The look of awe and sheer exhilaration on their faces make it worthwhile – and the best experiences are always better shared. The pilot won't object, unless the person is very heavy or particularly gauche which would slow everything down (and clumsy feet would definitely annoy the driver).

Pilots really can vary an enormous amount, as human beings do, but I have found from my experience that a flamboyant-but-experienced pilot is the best combination. Apart from being more fun they are more accommodating of your requests, regarding low-flying or difficult manoeuvres a challenge to their skills. I haven't yet met a helicopter pilot who didn't enjoy his work, and an excuse to display aerial expertise is often welcomed. Bending the rules slightly, to satisfy your requests, is often perfectly in order once away from the houses.

Having faith in your pilot obviously gives you considerable peace of mind when he's 'throwing it about' a little. I used to think that, if the engine stopped, all would plummet to the ground in a squishy mess, but this is not so. Even after obtaining their commercial flying licence, pilots have to take a competence test every six months, and part of the test is to prove their skill in coping with an engine failure. Following established procedures, they are able to 'feather' the helicopter safely to the ground. A reassuring thought! It wouldn't work if the rotors came off, but they are stringently made from the finest metals, making this eventuality so rare it can be discounted.

Back to the cockpit. In a four-seater there are two seats in the front, with the pilot usually sitting on the right-hand side. I know the forward view is better in the bubble at the front next to the pilot but, as a photographer, the best results are obtained by sitting immediately behind the pilot. Let your joy-riding friend sit up front, with his Walkman up full blast, playing "Bat Out of Hell" through the headphones. If you sit behind the pilot, he will see what you see, as he banks and turns, and vice versa. You will be able to identify target areas together and life will be so much easier for that. You are in constant touch through the headset, but be careful not to butt-in when he is listening, or talking, to ground control.

So there you are cruising at over 100 mph, overtaking everything in the fast lane on the motorway below you, arriving at your first target-area in amazingly quick time. Thanks to your pre-flight briefing with the pilot, you are within a mile of your site, and as he throttles back you either take over with verbal instruction, or work together to identify the target.

If you are in a restricted area you might only have permission for five minutes to get the job done and get out. Five minutes photography is quite a long time, if you are all "up-and-running" and ready to go. Don't think about it, but you are clocking up more than six pounds per minute and that's just the flying costs! If you have done your homework studying large-scale maps and plans, or have the advantage of having visited the site on the ground and discussed it fully with your client, you should have no trouble. The scene before you is just like a map, without the advantage of seeing place-names or signposts. One village looks very much the same as the next, one church just like another. The view you are seeing of towns is totally different to that at ground level. Here you are guided by railway lines, rivers and lakes. Major landmarks are your reference points and you have to relate them to points of the compass.

You discuss your thoughts with the pilot. You know which direction you came in from. You are looking for a property, north of the town's river, which backs onto a railway. You both look and circle. The more information you have, no matter how seemingly irrelevant, decides how quickly you find your objective. You compete to find it first, and you succeed. (So you should, you were there last week and have been studying it for days on the town plan). Fix the target in your mind's eye as soon as you identify it and before you lose it again. It's between a large sick-green roof and the river. Instruct your pilot to go to 1500 feet, circling the site as he does so. You can watch the play of light and shadows as you circle and mentally select your optimum viewpoints as discussed with the client. Keep an occasional eye on the altimeter, over the pilot's shoulder, so that you know what you're saying when you give instructions. Relate it to the scale of what's below you.

You've elected to use a normal angle lens first, at about 1000 feet. Pick your approach on a line that gives you the correct distance and height/ angle combination. You might misjudge it on the first run, being too far away, but take a picture anyway. Pilot don't expect any photographer to get it right all the time, so he circuits to take a line closer in, at the same height. Whilst you check your meter reading and camera settings he lines up for another run. This one's for real; you call out instructions.

"Keep it coming. Left a bit. Keep it coming. Looking good. Looking good. Now hold that line until I tell you to turn hard right." (I know it's 'starboard', but he understands English). "Looking good. Looking good." Picture. Picture. Picture. Picture. "OK, hard right!" You brace yourself, insulating the camera through your body, being careful not to let any part of the camera touch the vibrating airframe. Picture. Picture. Composing in the viewfinder as you go, you are happy that you have covered it from that height, with plenty of choices. You will notice that vibration increases with acceleration and decreases when the pilot throttles-back. And hovering is fun, but not as smooth as moving slowly. Now for some low-level stuff.

The field by the river is clear of children, and the grazing animals moved away to a corner soon after your arrival. There are no hospitals or electricity pylons nearby so, as already planned at briefing, you lose height by hovering in the ideal quarter; the optimum viewpoint angle. All buildings have one, seldom the rear of the property showing the dustbins. Pick the precise angle and distance to suit the wide-angle lens you have just fitted. Quick spot-meter reading off the brickwork, set camera controls, adjust polarising filter for maximum effect, focus. Picture. Down you go! Picture. Picture. Picture. "500 feet!", says the pilot, "and still losing height." Picture. Picture. "Forward a bit." Must beat the cloud-shadow approaching fast from the West. Picture. "Hold it there!"

Pilot says, "100 feet, be quick!" You reply, "Bit closer, please." Just to gain the perfect angle; the view you were hoping for comes out of nowhere, suddenly presenting itself. Picture. Picture. Last frame.

Pilot asks "OK?"

You yell "OK!", over the roar of wind and throb of rotors, without disguising a note of some triumph in your voice. Pilot pours on the power and pulls away from the buildings to gain height. Just as two-hundred waving factory workers flood out of the building to see what the rumpus is about.

You can't help returning a regal-salute, as you soar into the sun. Mission accomplished! You double-check your camera controls, and you know it's in the bag. You even allowed for the polariser that crisped up the colour contrast and cut through the slight haze of shooting almost into the light.

"Where to now?" says the pilot.

"Head ten miles north while I reload and check the maps."

Your girl friend lives there, en route to the next target, and right now she will be sun-bathing on the lawn next to the paddock. Landing on the paddock in a helicopter would be the posiest-ever way of 'arriving', putting a new meaning to the expression "dropping in".

Five minutes later, and with a reloaded camera fitted with a long lens, you direct your obliging pilot on a line that will put sunbathing-girlfriend neatly to your starboard side. You are in open country, and ask the pilot to make a fast pass at 150 feet, or less. There she is, still unaware of the impending intrusion. Camera ready, you rattle off half a dozen frames on motor-drive, just as she tries to cover her topless condition. Pilot is intrigued by your advance 'intelligence' and you explain that you could both pop back for tea and cakes on the lawn later; deciding to put your next target-site before that obvious pleasure. The present clear conditions cannot be taken for granted.

On beam, a further twenty miles to the north, lies a new commercial development being built on virgin land on the outskirts of a growing town. Your task is to obtain aerial photographs showing the current state of progress. These pictures will have several uses, including an overall record of all materials on-site and to illustrate photographically the present level of completion, or otherwise. The photographs could also be used in company literature to show a prestigious contract currently in hand.

So as not to waste valuable flying time you decide to add a few new shots to your ever-growing stock-library. You do this 'on the run' and this doesn't affect your pilot's progress in any way. He's talking to ATC anyhow, informing them of his forthcoming presence in their air-space. Not only polite, but necessary. Whilst he's getting clearance to operate at below 1500 feet in a country area west of the control zone, you make the most of the photo-opportunity to add mustard fields, meandering rivers, sleepy hamlets and a typical farmstead to your collection, allowing a couple of minutes approach time to reload before you start your final mission of the day.

So far, during this rather exciting sortie, you have been aware of the importance of 'keeping your cool'. There's a distinct danger that, with all this external stimulation bombarding your receptor cells, you can get over-excited and become over-awed with the occasion. This must not happen. A conscious effort may have to be made to keep your mind clear so that you can function at full efficiency. True, with the extra adrenalin pumping around your body, your mind will be sharp and all systems are at ready, but the trick is to maintain a calm exterior. This is best achieved by being constantly aware of your real part in the scenario. The reason for the charter-flight is for you to obtain photographs of certain sites. Nothing else; your enjoyment is an added bonus. The results are paramount and must be the main objective. Methodically using equipment that is totally familiar to you is your contact with normality. Calmly, and unhurriedly, going through your routines and camera checks, and monitoring the changing light. Be constantly aware of the need to consider certain filter additions. Warming up a hazy-blue scene, or purposely under or over-exposing by a fraction of a stop for effect. You know that you can relax later, but right now it's down to you, so hang in there and enjoy your work.

The last target comes into view and you confirm this with the pilot with whom you are now on first-name terms. You have decided to start at 2000 feet, and make right-hand circuits, spiralling down slowly. This way you cover all angles at varying heights, saving the close-up work until last. It's always quicker and smoother to lose height than to gain it. Because of the dust-haze you use a slightly-warm filter to prevent your transparencies having a too-blue cast, and decide to use the polariser again. You allow a stop-and-a-half, preferring your transparencies with full saturation. It's all going so smoothly you wonder if you have forgotten something. You might be getting too laid-back, you snatch a glance at all the camera's controls. No problems, but you're happier for checking. Camera-shake is the bane of an aerial photographers life, and you would rather be only one or two stops off maximum aperture than risk blurred pictures. With all those straps and cables around you, things can get moved accidentally sometimes.

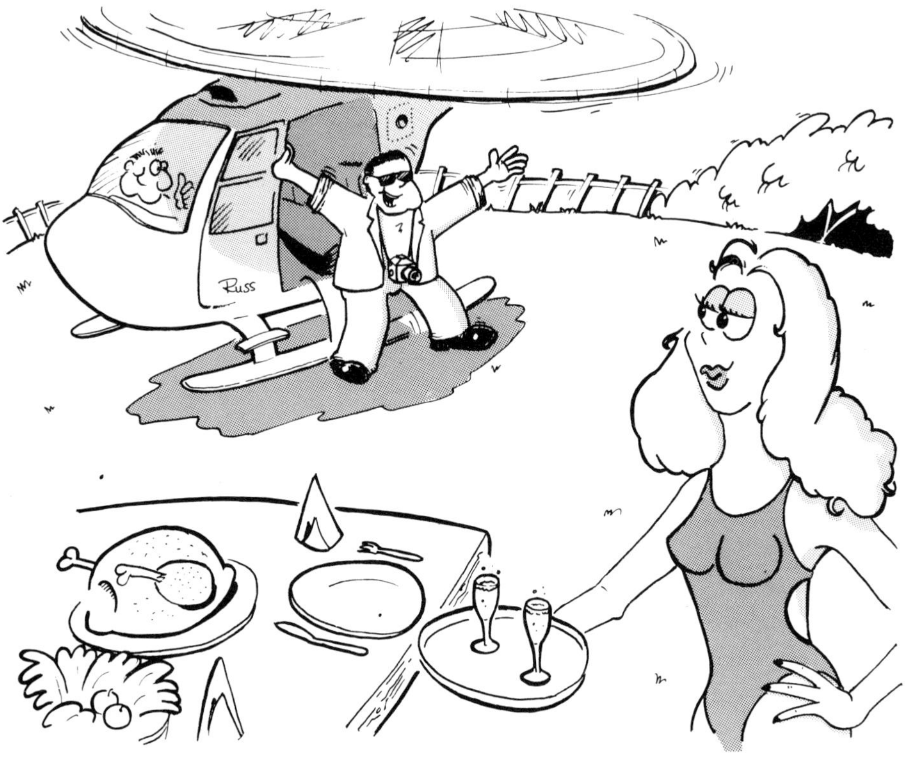

At the lower heights you remove the warming filter and put it in your shirt's top-pocket, noting that there could be a risk of dust-swirls from the rotors if you come too low. You have the authority to take pictures from the site contractors, but you should be considerate to the poor blighters working below. You bottom out at 100 feet, using up the currently loaded film and call out over the intercom, "Home James!" Once again the helicopter executes one of those posy action-man exits, leaving the workers on the ground wishing they weren't just laying bricks.

Time for afternoon tea and crumpets on the lawn!

NOTES

CHAPTER FOURTEEN.

A Mixture of Money and Art!

Final Reminder!

Becoming good at what you do and charging a reasonable fee for your professional services does not mean that you should not enjoy your work. On the contrary. If you are continually motivated in your work by a private desire to attain excellence you will enjoy the achievement, and what it can bring you both personally and financially. The personal success 'thing' we should now understand. It goes hand in hand with financial reward and, increased earning power, gives you the 'means whereby' you can further indulge in self-improvement. This might take the shape of more travel, or further investment in what you really want to do. If you spend your profits on equipment necessary to achieve better results, then that is justified investment in yourself and your own personal goals and, as such, can be offset against your tax when it becomes due.

When your earning power reaches the point where you earn more in a day than the average worker gets in a week, or even two weeks, you have special problems that may not seem like problems at first. Banking four-figure sums on a weekly or twice weekly basis may seem like utopia but careful money management is essential and, before things go too far, you should find an approachable, no-nonsense accountant with his feet firmly on terra firma. Tax can be avoided to a large extent, by clever spending, but tax cannot be evaded. Tax avoidance is legal. Tax evasion is not, and is punishable by law.

But earning money is not a sin, and clever management of that money really ought to become as familiar to you as f-stops. Not an obsession exactly, but a real awareness. If you want to 'join the club' you must follow certain rules and, without doubt, putting off the day that you have to come to terms with your tax obligations will only make matters worse. Doing nothing about your responsibilities will feel like having a vulture sitting on your shoulder; you will not be able to relax properly until you are totally organised. Far better to spend profits on your indulgences which are tax-allowable than to be faced with a tax-shocker in a year or two's time.

I am aware that some us dislike the idea of tax so much we will avoid even talking about it, and would rather read the telephone directory than study finance.

I am one of you, and can understand how you feel. This is why I purposely slipped this advice on tax into this mini-chapter, so that if you had skipped the financial section you wouldn't be totally ignorant in this department. But take heart, you are among friends. Just don't bury your head in the sand! Like all things in life, we only fear what we don't understand. Face the facts; we have a great job. And it gets better, proportionally, as we do ourselves. The rewards are fantastic. It can never be boring. You are your own boss and taskmaster. You are truly the champion of your own destiny. So enjoy!

A Question of Art?

Which is the odd one out? Chris Joyce, David Hamilton, Tim Graham or Helmut Newton? They are all photographers of some acclaim, with something *else* in common.

The quartet of talent which heads this section are all good at what they do, all dedicated to their art and will **all** be photographers for the rest of their lives, regardless of fame and recognition. They cannot help it!

It may not necessarily be their only interest in life, no more than it is mine but, it is what fires them and what they must do in life!

It makes them happy but it also makes them tired, frustrated and anxious. Through photography they 'feel' life, and work out their emotions and private thoughts. They don't have to explain why they do what they do, nor should they, even though they are elevated in their chosen speciality.

Their photographs are a statement for others to look upon and enjoy, but that which motivates each one of them is a personal and often private struggle to express themselves and leave the witnesses to their art wondering. Their 'audience' have their own reaction to the work, and each interpretation is equally private and personal.

Ask Tim Graham (the odd-one-out) why he almost tirelessly strives for those elusive images of Royalty, as he clatters his Nikons and long-lenses that dangle around his slight frame. Competing, as he does, with an entourage of photographers for the best Royal pictures in all weathers, globe-trotting to chase his personal goals of excellence in what he chooses to do. Often asking himself, "Why?" as his punishing, self-imposed struggle for achievement exhausts him!

Tim is doubtless an 'achiever' but he doesn't see it that way, and can never sit back on his laurels when there is so much he feels he must do. He drives himself on for his art!

As do Chris Joyce, Helmut Newton and David Hamilton. Each with their own style but with a common objective which practically haunts them. Though they do other things, they are all drawn to photographing the female form. Helmut Newton, now in his 'senior years' and world-acclaimed for his sensual 'fashion' shots and calendars, admits even though he is 'comfortably off' he can't put his camera away, and probably never will! His personal style and special view of women is well-known, and almost a 'signature' we all recognise. When questioned, Mr Newton defends his work, maintaining that most photographers are 'voyeurs' of a sort; and he's right!

How else can we effectively do what we do if we are not the "watchers of the world" ? We are the observers and photo-scribes of our day, cursed, blessed or gifted to record life as we see it! And, whether we are paid to do it or not, we should still be doing it!

Those that photograph machinery, and do pack-shots of shoddy plastic goods, do it because they are good at it and are paid well in return. We have an unwritten a code of honour that makes us strive to record and sometimes glamourise.

We look at life, and everything around us, in an entirely different light to everyone else; and we honestly can't help it!

When my clients hear that I have been photographing female models for some 'tasteful' promotion, their minds go straight to sex; and that is a common misconception for 'outsiders'. I stopped explaining many years ago, that even when photographing naked people, it has nothing to do with 'sex'. Suffering their 'nudge nudge, wink wink' comments, I merely let them think whatever they want to think. Sure, as a man, I can appreciate an attractive girl, and still see in them that which others do; but we see beyond carnality (most of the time).

Try explaining to a maiden Aunt you are only interested in 'form' or 'light and shade', and she will only see it as an excuse to leer at a naked body, and could even leave you seriously wondering about your true motives!

Personally, I think our outlook on life, and people, is even more fulfilled because we *can* separate the opposite gender from sex. They are separate issues to us, and we are much healthier for it.

Possibly, deep down, our appreciation of the female form *could* be rooted in that god-given gift to find another person physically fascinating (to encourage us to procreate), but the beauty we see therein inspires us to record those secret shadows and the sensual sheen of skin which has been tantalising artists since man had the urge to paint on cave walls!

Our cameras are ingeniously manipulated by us to capture those 'slices of life', as did Gauguin with his oils. We may not see his Tahitian models for what they truly were, but we see them how he interpreted them. Without their odours or the sweetness of their breath and winsome ways, they are still charming. Had Gauguin lived in today's world he would have definitely been a photographer, forsaking his clutter of canvas and oils in his relentless efforts to preserve for posterity.

I know how he must have felt, and the hundreds of others just like him, that have volunteered their lives to this pursuit – in the name of art.

FINIS

NOTES

Acknowledgements.

My ideas, formed during my professional life, can only be opinion, based upon observation and personal interpretation, but there is much sound evidence to support each philosophy which has been thoroughly tried and tested in the field.

Just as honest musicians must admit their creativity has been inspired by those gone before, I, likewise, acknowledge my mentors. My own sources of inspiration are many and varied, and some personal acknowledgements are listed below.

Emile Couee
Al Koran
Dr Maxwell Maltz MD
Karsh of Ottawa
David Bailey
Terence Donovan
Richard Sadler
Helmut Newton
Jon Davison
Chris Joyce
David Hamilton
Tim Graham

Not forgetting,

Joseph Niepce
Charles Chevalier
Louis Daguerre
for their dedication in the 19th Century.

NOTES